Praise for *Nasty Women*

'An essential window into many of the hazard-strewn worlds younger women are living in right now.'
– Margaret Atwood, author of *The Handmaid's Tale* (Twitter)

'An important if not essential collection of essays, this book is almost impossible to put down. It will make you proud to call yourself a nasty woman.'
– Louise O'Neill, author of *Asking For It*

'An essential, incredible multitudinous riot of voices… required reading.'
– Nikesh Shukla, editor of *The Good Immigrant*

'This is a stunning collection of essays: moving, brutal and searingly honest. *Nasty Women* makes for powerful, essential reading. Everyone should read this inspiring book.'
– Cat Clarke, author of *The Lost and the Found*

'*Nasty Women* Is The Intersectional Essay Collection Feminists Need' – The Huffington Post

'In the face of bigotry comes a collection of powerful essays.'
– The List

'Sizzling hot, radical, and a great solace.'
– Chitra Ramaswamy, author of *Expecting*

'This is a stunning collection that in turn made my heart break, then soar. Compelling, essential reading.'
– Sarah Mason, Programme Manager, The Saltire Society

NASTY WOMEN

A COLLECTION of ESSAYS + ACCOUNTS
ON WHAT IT IS TO BE A WOMAN
IN THE 21ST CENTURY

Published by 404 Ink
www.404ink.com
@404Ink

ISBN: 978-0-9956238-2-8
ebook: 978-0-9956238-3-5

Cover design: Maria Stoian

Editors: Laura Jones & Heather McDaid

Printed and bound in Great Britain
by Clays Ltd, St Ives plc

CONTENTS

DEAR NASTIES OF
THE WORLD,

THIS IS AN

TELL YOUR STORIES

AND TELL THEM
LOUD

INDEPENDENCE DAY

Katie Muriel

They are calling him my president, and I am scared out of my mind. They are calling him my president, and there is bile in my throat as they ask me to respect him. They are calling him my president, and each time I think about it my chest feels tight with indignation, or rage, or an impending sense of doom. I can no longer tell these feelings apart and I think they've evolved into something I can't entirely give voice to, something that tastes all the more sour each day when I wake up and find that it wasn't just a vivid nightmare. They are calling him my president and my future has never seemed so bleak.

I can't recall the last time I looked on my country with pride. I know that it was when I still counted my age in the single digits, but I couldn't give you an exact year. Born on our Independence Day and given the middle name Liberty, a much younger version of me used to stand tall with an immense sense of faux patriotism at the sound of my full name. I glowed with delight at the fireworks that graced every birthday; my heart burst along with them. I knew that words like 'freedom' and 'courage' seemed synonymous with the name of my country, and, for a long time, I trusted these ideals blindly in the way only a child trusts.

Late in the evening of the 8th of November 2016, when it first became apparent that Donald J. Trump was going to win the American presidency, I learned, for perhaps the millionth time since that distant starry-eyed childhood, what it is to feel shame for my nation. That night is unforgettable. I remember a tense, unearthly quiet broken only now and then by distant, vague cries of 'No!' from unidentifiable places in my vicinity.

Any other day, this might have seemed comically overdramatic, ridiculously cinematic, but right then, it felt like what it was: grief. It was as gut-wrenching as it might have been if everyone around me had just discovered someone they loved had quite suddenly died. In the hours before this, we convinced ourselves that it couldn't happen, that it wasn't possible. Slowly, the tallies came in, reality took hold, and I sat alone in my room, in a country not my own, one month from the end of my study abroad programme, trying to come to grips with the idea that I would soon have to return home. I would have to return to my own country that, like others before it, was now destined to fall under the rule of a racist, misogynistic demagogue.

It wasn't as though I had thought America immune. It wasn't as though I cast a condescending eye on 'those other places' that had seen the lives of their citizens turned upside down time and again by political leaders whose ideologies were uncomfortable at best and fatal at worst. The United States *has* had terrible Presidents before, and at the risk of sounding cynical, will have them again when Trump has had his time. It was a naïve part of me that saw Trump do and say such horrible things, witnessed his complete lack of capability and worthiness to lead, and thought that even the most reprehensible people in my country would, at the last second, understand that allowing this would not 'Make America Great Again.' It would merely reveal the nasty, rotting heart of America that I daresay it has always had since it built a throne on stolen land and tried to crown itself king of the world.

Much of my family supports Trump. Truthfully, this came as little surprise given that many of them are conservative Protestants, and conservative values and Republicans tend to be bosom buddies. I begrudge nobody their faith; I, too, have a faith in which I strongly believe, and because I love my family, I know that I can co-exist with them even when we disagree. I would be lying if I said that it doesn't hurt when members of my family espouse political beliefs that ultimately disparage the existence of others, but I try my best to keep the peace. Sometimes, however, peace has to take a holiday. Sometimes, there are battles to be fought.

Four days after the election, in the midst of trying to process my disbelief, I was dealt another blow, this one far more personal.

I knew my aunt to be a Trump supporter, and for a long time, as with most of the people I encountered on Facebook who ate, slept, and breathed Donald J. Trump in the last year, I tried to ignore this. *Family is family*, I told myself, remembering that I had once forgiven this very same aunt, my mother's sister, for directing an ethnic slur at me. In hindsight, that was very telling, but we had long moved on from that incident. Starting a war within my family meant drama I didn't need, and so in the months preceding the election and in the hours after, I did my best to turn my head away, grit my teeth, and bite the virtual tongue that longed to say something, anything.

To my credit, I held out until the Friday following the election, when I could no longer bear it. In what I thought was a fair and balanced response to a startlingly ignorant post this aunt had shared on Facebook, I asked – begged, even – for her to see things from the perspective of all those who, under the looming shadow of Trump's reign, now feared for their right to live, or even exist, as free citizens of the United States. Satisfied that I had made points she could not possibly disagree with, I put my phone away and went about my day. Later that night, after hours of back-and-forth Facebook discussion I tried to stay away from, I received a message from my mother full of copied and pasted comments from my aunt. Among them: *With her attitude she comes off more like a spic than anything*.

There it was. That word again. For those unaware, the word 'spic' is an ethnic slur typically aimed at those of Latinx descent. I, being mixed Puerto Rican, had been deemed deserving of this slur by my white aunt. She had decided I was *too big for my britches*. I had a smart mouth that, in her opinion, I needed to stop running. She had discovered in the past that aiming this slur at me was an effective way to silence me and years ago, when she first threw the insult at me, I was indeed silenced. For a moment, when she again referred to me with this word, I felt the same hurt, the same fragility. But only for a moment.

Maybe she didn't know, as many of my other family members likely don't, that in the years since the first time she called me 'spic', I have spent a lot of time exploring my identity. I often ask myself, *What does it mean to be mixed? How do I identify with the Puerto Rican people from whom I descend? Why do people who are only white have trouble with the idea that being 'mixed with white' doesn't make you white?* When I examined the words my aunt typed to my mother, as well as the interaction that followed in which I confronted my aunt, it became clear to me that she was disgusted with what she perceived to be my lack of recognition of the white people I also descend from. My focus on finding the part of myself to which I have always had less access – in other words, my discovery and display of Latinx pride – meant that, to her, I did not live up to her standard of the whiteness I possess but do not feel the need to celebrate. Setting aside for the moment the disturbing notion of white pride, this aunt decided that if I wanted to deny my whiteness (something I have never done, as it risks perpetuating colourism), she would boast to me about how her white child would naturally see more success than I ever will, because I am a spic and, to quote her, *a spic is PR trash.*

Trash. She told me I am trash. Trash made apparently trashier by virtue of being Puerto Rican trash. If you squint hard enough, you can see how ludicrous it all is, but more often than not I have to laugh so I don't cry. It's not really the pain of the word 'spic' itself, nor does it shock me beyond sense that she should call me this when it has happened once before. History repeats, as they say. No, it's that she accepted my forgiveness the first time, spent years acting as though all was well and, at the first opportunity, revealed that she has clearly thought this of me all along. Trump's election nudged this into light and, for whatever reason, it is this that stings the most.

This is not the first nor is it the last family divide Trump will leave in his wake, but I refuse to think of him as some deity who idly shifts pieces on a board in his golden war room. He has an inflated sense of himself but ultimately, I know that he is not the singular cause of this split in my family. It existed long before he opened the shark's maw he calls a mouth and proclaimed he was going to run for President. What I do know is that he significantly widened the gap. He used the power he has always had to place his hands where they didn't belong, and he boasted about it. He happily ignited and fuelled racial stereotypes. He ostracised an entire religion. He took advantage of anything in life there was to take advantage of and laughed about it. In doing all of this he inserted himself into the fissures that radiated through my family and made them canyons.

It was never a matter of opinion versus opinion, because as we are all taught from a young age, opinion does not stand up to fact. Proclaiming that Trump isn't a racist or a misogynist or a liar or a cheater when the opposite has been proven a hundred times over does not simply make it so. It hurts to see, in particular, female members of my family support him. I do not understand how a woman can hear 'I just start kissing them' and 'Grab them by the pussy' and think him anything other than disgusting. I do not understand how so many of them can deem him fit to be anything more than dirt on the ground, let alone the President of the United States of America. This isn't because I am under the impression that all women share the same needs, values, beliefs, or experiences, but because the survivor I am wanted to believe that the majority of the population believe sexual assault is reprehensible. It is clear that I was wrong, and I am terrified by how so many people normalised this behaviour and made it acceptable by voting it into my country's highest political office.

It is important for me to note that of Trump's potential victims I am not at the most risk – and yes, we are potential victims, as we have and will face direct harm as a result of his policies. My skin is a few shades darker than many of my friends, but about a dozen shades lighter than my father's. I'm a brown girl, but not *that* brown of a brown girl. My Spanish is so pitiful as to be nearly non-existent, and I am conditionally white passing on nine days out of ten. I have Latinx relatives that are darker than I am, and Black relatives that are certainly darker than I am. I have Black, Latinx, and Muslim friends who do not now simply fear for their livelihoods but their actual *lives*. I shake in terror for them and with them and I cannot decide what is scarier: that Trump is President, or that people I know and love enabled him. What I *have* decided is that my aunt was right about one thing: I have a damn big mouth, and I'm going to use it.

The word 'spic' will no longer silence me. Yes, my hair is wild and bears a distinctly Afro-Latinx texture, and I have only learned in the last few years, when I began to learn love for myself, that the way it curls and kinks is uniquely *of colour*. Yes, my nose is perhaps a little wider than average, and there's a patch of much darker skin on the thick curve of my left hip that looks as though whatever force created me decided this was enough melanin. I am proud of all of these things. I love my mother, I love who she is and where she comes from, but there are non-white features on my face and my body and I have learned to love them, too. I am a half-breed, I am a spic, and to quote a John Leguizamo character in a phrase I have grown particularly fond of, 'I am spictacular!'

But I'm still scared. I don't know what comes next. Simply saying the words 'Trump's America' sends icy shivers up and down my spine. I cast my eyes towards history and I can pick out moment after moment when white supremacy was allowed to rip land away from the Indigenous, make slaves of Black people, segregate a nation and without irony still call it 'United.' I look to the very recent past and find that white supremacy enabled a rapist to get six months and only serve three, killed dozens of young Black men and allowed almost every police officer behind the trigger to escape without charges, tore up sacred Native land to line its pockets. It feels like years ago we thought Trump was a joke, then we blinked and white supremacy elected a white supremacist to the office who appointed a cabinet of more white supremacists. It is cyclical, it does not end, and tomorrow another woman will have her hijab torn off in the street, another child will see her parents deported, another young Black man will be wrongly booked into prison.

The divides in my country have always existed, and they hurt. The divides in my family have always existed, and they too hurt. I look at my identities – woman, Latinx, survivor – and I can draw an arrow from each and point towards dozens of ways a Trump presidency has already and will continue to simply *hurt* me. But I know what courage is now. I know what freedom means. They are not words synonymous with the name of my country because its name is boldly untrue and stained with the blood of those who really built it. No, they are words synonymous with my country's most marginalised people, the ones who stand in the face of brutal opposition and know that backing down is not an option. The ones who know they will someday take this country back. The ones who know that true patriotism is not a song or a flag or the face of an old, dead white man carved into a mountainside.

A long time ago, I didn't understand the point of Independence Day. It used to be a history lesson, and for most people, it probably still is. But for me, every day is now Independence Day. Every day that I embrace the parts of myself I have been denied is my day of freedom from oppressive rule. Every day that I turn the word 'spic' over my tongue, I claim another day of liberty. *That* is the point. You best believe that I am still scared, and this is not the last day of fear. But I'm proclaiming here and now that this is my Independence Day. He is not my president. Anyone that thinks I'm Puerto Rican trash is free to do so as long as they also note one final thing: I am goddamn *spictacular*.

WHY I'M NO LONGER A PUNK ROCK 'COOL GIRL'

Kristy Diaz

I'm at a punk show in the city I live in and I'm talking to one of the bands. They're friends of mine, and we're chatting about the interview we did a few months ago. The promoter comes over, who is also in one of the bands playing the show. I don't know him but I recognise him.

He comes over and asks me who I am, accusingly.

'Are you from Leicester? How do *you* know these guys?'

I'm flustered and confused and fall ungracefully over my words. Yes, I'm from Leicester, these guys are my friends.

He goes on to motion to someone behind me and tells me not to worry, he's not looking at my tits and having been thrown by the earlier interrogation, I tell him with regained confidence that I know, they're not on my head, which is where he was looking.

Over the past 15 years of going to shows I've had fights, I've been groped, I've got scars earned in mosh pits, and I've fallen face down on wooden floors.

And yet, this is the most intimidated I've ever been at a show. A reminder that, as a woman in punk, you constantly need to defend yourself against challenges of space, ownership, and identity to justify that you're cool enough to be standing where you are.

★ ★ ★

The 'cool girl' is a concept coined in a book I've never read (Gillian Flynn's *Gone Girl*) but became familiar with through feminist and pop culture writing.[1] It describes a particular trope of woman that seems to exist to satisfy the desires of men – she shares their interests, is attractive but low-maintenance, is basically 'one of the guys'.

> *'Men always say that as the defining compliment, don't they? She's a cool girl.'*
>
> *'Cool Girls never get angry; they only smile in a chagrined, loving manner and let their men do whatever they want. Go ahead, shit on me, I don't mind, I'm the Cool Girl. Men actually think this girl exists. Maybe they're fooled because so many women are willing to pretend to be this girl.'*

I was the punk rock version of the 'cool girl' trope for years.

The punk rock 'cool girl' likes *real* music. *Good* music. *Proper* music. She's into the latest hot hardcore band playing to fifteen people right now. She knows every word to *The Shape of Punk to Come*. She doesn't listen to pop music, or dance music, or stuff that Other Girls like. Her favourite Braid record is the Correct One. She only sings along to Panic! At The Disco, ironically. She can hang out with your musician mates and hold her own in a conversation, but she won't point out the ways in which even punk rock, this glorious utopia we inhabit, has the capacity to oppress.

And, much like the original concept, she's not real.

She loves music. That *is* real, to the point that it defines her. But she's learned the performative nature of punk fandom, the language we use to talk about which bands we're allowed to like, and which ones we aren't. She knows that liking the 'wrong' bands will make her less credible. She exists within a set of boundaries, and edits herself accordingly.

---

1   Adewunmi, Bim. 'I used to scorn 'cool girls', but now see they don't really exist', *The Guardian*, 17 September 2012. www.theguardian.com/commentisfree/2012/sep/17/cool-girl-gone-girl.

★ ★ ★

Being a woman involved in punk in any capacity is an exercise in navigating a constant, shifting set of hypocrisies. Often, it's the microaggressions that ring loudest.

The fear of being labelled a 'fangirl', or a 'poser', or a 'scene kid' runs deep; heavily gendered insults thrown in the MySpace era I grew up in. This didn't stop me from levelling them at other women. The women I wasn't like.

Internalised sexism manifested in ugly ways, from disguising my own femininity and sneering at women who wore heels to shows. The entitlement of identity and wanting ownership over music, dismissing others as scenesters who weren't serious about music. Mirroring the behaviours of men.

Consider the ways in which women are treated, however, and this becomes a logical but destructive defence mechanism. Armour against the onslaught of expectations. Expectations that you'll have the right networks, know the bands, the promoters, the labels, but can't hang out with your friends at a show without your status being questioned.

Expectations that you'll wear the right band T-shirts. Project onto other women instead of pointing out the irony of articles calling out hardcore bands for being meatheads whilst declaring that the definitive sign of their succumbing to the mainstream is a conventionally attractive woman wearing their T-shirt at a gym.[2]

However, at one point in time I'd have said exactly the same thing. I'd have thought she was a poser who got into hardcore whilst it was trendy. I had listened to so much bullshit that I believed it.

It isn't just hardcore. The narrative surrounding 'real emo', whilst often well-meaning and with legitimate arguments about

2   Rosenberg, Axl. 'Todd Jones from Nails is a Scene Bully', *Metal Sucks*, 27 June 2016. www.metalsucks.net/2016/06/27/todd-jones-from-nails-scene-bully/.

the media persistently conflating 'emo' with 'guitar music that is sad', has perpetuated an exclusivity that has been hard to shake off. It took me an embarrassing amount of time to reconcile my love of the genre across its 'waves', as though knowing your history meant you couldn't enjoy your present.

Your music knowledge is going to constantly come into question, though, so make sure you've read up. The very coolest of cool girls are being 'taught' about music. Invisible, malleable girlfriends who need to be educated about the right bands.

These unsolicited recommendations exist everywhere, from online discussions to entire songs. For example, in Moose Blood's 'Bukowski', the language used is one-way, the subject completely passive.

I'll introduce you *to Clarity*
Teach you *the words to The Sound of Settling*
Make you *watch High Fidelity*

There are plenty of lyrics like this, and from some of my all-time favourite bands. I had to go back to Brand New's *Your Favourite Weapon* and Glassjaw's 'Everything You Ever Wanted To Know About Silence' and really reflect on some of those lyrics.

It is a difficult position to take when the music you love contributes to something you don't. But, for me, being able to examine it critically played the biggest role in stepping out of the 'cool girl' trope.

It allowed me to realise that other women are not the problem. Like me, they are also having their credibility questioned, being sidelined as the voiceless subjects of songs, and being indirectly told that the music they are so deeply passionate about is selected based on who they are sleeping with, or want to sleep with. That they are always one badly curated mixtape away from knowing anything about music.

Kristy Diaz

* * *

As a DJ at a successful club night I found myself up against countless men every week telling me that I wasn't good at my job. Whilst playing to a packed dance floor, they would ask 'Why are you playing this? No-one likes it.'

Play my request.

Give me your number.

This song is shit.

It didn't matter if I was playing Q And Not U or Girls Aloud. They would never be appeased. It wasn't Shellac, or the Stone Roses, and I was still a woman. I couldn't gain the level of respect I so desperately wanted. I had to stop trying.

Being the 'cool girl' is not a solution. It is a parasitic distraction, and it takes away from everything else about you. Reduces you to a record collection. Highly unrecommended. Zero stars.

It's okay to be uncool. Forget the notion of cool, and forget the notion of cool as defined by anyone else other than yourself. One of the most liberating things I've unlearned is looking for the approval of men, and since abandoning those constraints I enjoy music more. I can allow myself to not like things I feel I 'should' like. I embrace all of my wide-ranging tastes. I listen to infinitely more music made by women than I did ten years ago. I'm learning to stop comparing myself to other women, and viewing them as competition.

Let that shit go. Never deny yourself the music you enjoy. Sing and scream along with every breath. Collaborate with women and other marginalised groups in punk, rally around each other, protect and support each other and invest energy in creating. Never apologise for an inch of space you occupy and answer to no-one. Fuck it up at DIY shows and dance to pop music recklessly, wearing heels and glitter and jeans and cut up T-shirts. Be taught nothing. You know everything.

'Why I'm No Longer A Punk Rock 'Cool Girl'' was first published by Track 7 *in January 2017:* www.trackseven.net. *Editor: Jade Curson.*

BLACK FEMINISM ONLINE: CLAIMING DIGITAL SPACE

Claire L. Heuchan

I write as a Black woman. That's nothing new – I've been writing since the first time I picked up a pencil in primary one. Yet, me speaking as a Black woman is a point of interest, both to my supporters and detractors, to the extent that my position has become significant in itself.

It's a curious thing, to consider what having voice as a Black woman means. Every single act, every last word and deed, I carry out as a Black woman. Being Black and female, that's fairly unavoidable. I make a cup of tea as a Black woman. I drive my car into town as a Black woman. I have spent around 300 hours playing *Fallout: New Vegas* as a Black woman (both me and the character representing me – customisable character creation is very much appreciated). These aspects of everyday life as a Black woman generally pass unnoticed by wider society, with the exception of a few basement-dwelling Redditors who consider the availability of non-white, non-male video game protagonists to be the height of political correctness gone mad.

The mundane and the personal elements of life as a Black woman in British society are, for the most part, not controversial. That isn't to say it's perfect. Women of colour are disproportionately impacted by austerity[1], less likely to be hired than our white and/or female peers, and on average paid less than them even when we get the job. Black and female bodies are fetishised, treated like public property by the white men who

---

1   *Minority Women and Austerity,* www.minoritywomenandausterity.com

grope us on the assumption Black girls are always up for it. Black women are routinely Othered by the white women who touch our hair without permission or preamble, acting like natural hair is a curiosity and the Black women growing it are attractions at the petting zoo.

Black women are bombarded with reminders – both subtle and overt – that we do not fit. We live with an undercurrent of British nationalism, fostered by the politics of Brexit, which considers Black and British identities to be mutually exclusive. This can manifest in a number of ways, like the assumption that Black and brown people must *originally* be from a country outside of the United Kingdom. Every time a stranger persists in questioning where I'm really from, the truth – that I was born in Glasgow – is met with a palpable layer of incredulity. It's like a less funny mirror image of that iconic scene in *Mean Girls* when Karen asks Cady '…but if you're from Africa, why are you white?' Often, the stranger then tries to calculate a combination of words that will get me to reveal why I'm simultaneously Black and British without making them sounding racist. And every time they fail, for one simple reason: it *is* racist. The idea that Black must mean Other is fundamentally racist in its logic.

Scotland is a fairly isolating place to be a Black woman. There are more churches within a mile radius of my home than houses inhabited by other people of colour. We are scattered. I think that Black girls here are treated as anomalies – because there are relatively few of us, white people act like we're lone exceptions. If our presence is a simple one-off, then Black women and girls don't need to be recognised as a group. We are dismissed as a collective unit. And if we are atomised, considered a discrepancy rather than a pattern in our own right, our place in Scottish society remains unacknowledged. Black women are made invisible here – not always, but often enough that it is hard to see ourselves reflected in Scottish community.

It's difficult to find a sense of belonging in a place we are considered more Other than of. The traditional solution is to move to London. There's an assumption that follows creative women of colour in Scotland: sooner or later we will tire of how conspicuous our melanin makes us and head south. So far, I have resisted the siren call of London. It's great to arrive there and be one of many Black women in the train carriage, to blend in, but it's also lovely to get home to Glasgow and leave the grim urgency of London behind.

Jackie Kay, our Poet Makar, is firmly connected to this country. She is so intrinsically Scottish in her humour, her easy warmth, that it is impossible to imagine otherwise. Kay's writing is a perfect articulation of what it is to be Scottish. It's also the purest expression I've ever found of what it is to be a Black woman who is Scottish. Like her, I can't conceive of a life entirely separate from Scotland. But without the digital revolution, I'm not entirely sure that I'd feel the same way.

Like many kids growing up in a small town, I spent an introspective childhood dreaming that the excitement of real life would begin when I left. Adventure and creativity were assumed to be the preserve of those living a city life. Upon reaching maturity, I was going to go off in pursuit of the music, the literary scene, the art, that flourished in places I had only imagined visiting. This vibrant cultural world capable of nourishing me could surely only exist somewhere bigger, somewhere better than my tiny coastal town.

At the age of twelve I would save up my pocket money, go online, order albums from obscure record labels, and wait weeks for them to be shipped over from America. Getting home from school and checking the post for those parcels, holding incontrovertible proof in my hands that the world I was waiting to step into was actually real, it was a special kind of magic. Then MP3s happened and that world got closer still, if less tangible. It could be accessed in an instant (provided our internet connection was stable). The immediacy of the digital revolution made a whole host of things that had felt unimaginable suddenly possible.

There was also, in my head, an idea that I'd find and live in a place with more Black people – possibly the United States of America. At that age, the stark reality of police brutality and confederate pride hadn't yet sunk in and I was still enamoured of the American dream, the mythic equality of opportunity that meant anyone could belong if they were prepared to work hard enough.

That's not to say the UK is dramatically better. The stiff upper-lip repressiveness of British society, the narrative of exceptionalism that enables Scotland to think of itself as fairer than the rest of the UK, mean we are yet to unpick the nation's colonial legacy. Sheku Bayoh, Sarah Reed, Joy Gardner, Mark Duggan, Cherry Groce, and too many other Black men and women have died at police hands for us to pretend that state-sanctioned, anti-Black racism only happens on the other side of the Atlantic Ocean. All I knew then, though I hardly dared acknowledge it, was that I wanted to be somewhere that whiteness wasn't ubiquitous, taken as the expected standard of humanity.

Gaining internet access changed a great deal more than I first realised. The first few years of my life were spent with four accessible television channels, and the addition of a fifth was seen as rather exotic by my family (although my grandmother and I did enjoy watching *Home and Away* together on Channel 5). There wasn't a great deal of choice to be had in media available to consume, and what was there scarcely alluded to any Black British reality – the closest I came to seeing representation was Heather Small of *M People* performing on Top of the Pops. And then just a few clicks of a mouse opened up a whole new realm of possibilities, made them all available in my home.

I could watch hair tutorials made by other Black girls on YouTube. I could read words written by Black women, find our stories with far greater ease than I would during fruitless hours of flicking through a newspaper or magazine. Hearing of books that weren't on the school curriculum, in the local library, or acknowledged by literary supplements – books by Black authors

– became a far more straightforward process. There was an AOL chat room for Black people in Britain that quickly became my favourite corner of the internet – the words 'Black' and 'British' were in its official title, and that recognition brought its own extraordinary thrill. And it wasn't necessary to leave the house in order to access any of this, never mind the confines of my small Scottish town. It wasn't the same as being surrounded by enough Black people offline to be visually unremarkable, but it is still an acknowledgement that makes a difference. Time was limited – at first because of the expense of our dial-up connection, and then because my grandfather got tired of me hogging the desktop computer – but the opportunity was there, and it was a revelation.

At 16 I got my first laptop and began writing prolifically. Nothing I wrote was even slightly political (which is just as well because my politics were woefully underdeveloped), unless you count the consistent representation of lesbian relationships in my many works of *Harry Potter* fanfiction. My blog Sister Outrider was still years away. But without the internet it seems far less likely that I'd imagine myself, a black sheep (pun fully intended) with no obvious place in society, as someone who had anything worth saying or writing. The internet was the first place I ever witnessed Black women being properly heard, our voices and our words engaged with, in a public setting. With the development of digital media, it became much easier to access content and to participate in conversations relevant to me as a Black woman.

Reflecting on my relationship with digital space, it seems inevitable that I would find my voice online and turn to blogging. Academics and activists alike have observed that women of colour are creating platforms for ourselves, platforms that did not previously exist, and gaining traction through the democracy of new media. Having a voice in a digital setting frequently results in traditional media sources – print, radio, journalism, television – enabling women of colour to address even larger audiences than we do through our social media presence or as part of the feminist blogosphere. These engagements can even pay some of the bills. Our skills and cultural contributions are more readily recognised online, where we can make space for them. The plurality of the internet makes it a more viable space for women of colour. There are more options available – what to watch, what to click, what to pay for – meaning that consumption need not be passive. We are able to support one another.

Certain doors were once largely closed to us due to the gatekeeping of old media. It's not a neutral act, providing or withholding a platform. It's a decision actively made: whose voice to amplify and whose voice to ignore. In the last few years there has been much talk of 'diversity' in relation to the media – and talk is often as much as it amounts to.

Diversity often means business as usual: a white team with the addition of one or two brown people. No difficult questions about why those with the power to hire or commission are almost entirely white, and what that means in terms of whose stories they consider worth telling. No awkward speculation about which perspectives are valued and which are not, how the organisation reached this point and found only white people with a seat at the table. The situation remains the same, unexamined at the root, with a little garnish of colour that allows those making decisions to pat themselves on the back over how progressive they are. Dr Karen Salt describes diversity as 'the sprinkle approach', devoid of any structural change.

What I like best about new media is that it has the potential to be different, a potential which is often converted into reality through the innovative work done by people of colour online. Samantha Asumadu, a Black woman, is the founding editor of Media Diversified – a news site with content written entirely by people of colour. Tobi Oredein, a Black woman, created and successfully crowdfunded the publication Black Ballad after pointing out that the avocado got more attention in magazines geared towards women than anything geared towards Black and female experience. Siana Bangura, a Black woman, curates No Fly on the Wall, an organisation devoted to highlighting and celebrating the work of Black women. These women, and others like them, are pioneers. Using digital space creatively can enact powerful change.

When I started to write as Sister Outrider, it felt entirely experimental. I had a reasonable Twitter presence (it's @ClaireShrugged if you want to hit me up) and plenty to say. My ideas had influence, gained traction. But I wanted to make them permanent in a way a Twitter thread isn't, provide an accessible resource for people to learn about Black feminism instead of having the same conversations over and over again. For ages I held off on the assumption that someone more qualified was going to come along and say it all, that I didn't necessarily have the right or insight required to speak up. But nobody ever did say the exact things I believed needed to be said, at least not in the feminist spaces I was occupying online or offline, and while I waited the same patterns of casual racism in a feminist context kept repeating themselves. So I created Sister Outrider.

Blogging was free. It meant I got to write more, something I had always loved. The worst that could happen, I reasoned, was that nobody would read my posts. But people do read them. Thousands of people, from all around the world. One essay has been translated into Portuguese by Vulva Revolução, discussed by Brazilian feminists. What I had to say about race and feminism resonated. Women began writing to me privately with questions. They also send their thanks to me for affirming that they are not alone, which is incredibly humbling, or tell me that my writing helped them learn something, which is the most rewarding feedback possible.

Of course, with visibility comes abuse. That is the case for all women, and doubly true for Black women. Along with the misogyny, there is a persistent racism that shapes both the content and frequency of our abuse online. There is no way to deal with the racial slurs, the graphic racist images, the violent threats – at least, none that I have found. It's scary. It hurts. It stays with you after you turn off your phone, close your laptop.

It is no coincidence that when I speak, when I hold a set of views and am vocal about them in the public arena, that my Black womanhood becomes a source of ire. It is the presence of Black women in a public life that remains contentious, that draws all kinds of harassment. That's the case in digital or physical spaces. Diane Abbott, the first Black woman to be elected as a member of the British Parliament, is hounded because of who she is rather than what she actually does in her capacity as politician. Instead of a cause for celebration, her career is treated like a joke by the conservative right and the white feminist left alike, the punchline reliant on misogynoir.[2] What I find particularly ironic is that those who despise us simply for being Black and female are often the fiercest critics of identity politics.

Cyberfeminism had this idea, at the outset of the digital revolution, that the internet would foster connections between people that reached beyond the barriers of structural inequalities like gender, race, or social class. It was egalitarian, in a naïve sort of way, this presumption that material bodies would cease to shape interactions online – that the meeting of minds in shared digital spaces would overcome the differences separating our human exteriors, the factors preventing us from finding common ground in the analogue world, and build connections detached from structural power imbalances. Sadly, this was nothing more than a pipe dream.

The abuse lessens when I change my avatar from a photograph of myself to a picture of a cartoon character. Other women of colour switch to dogs or stock images for respite. And that's because this abuse is sent with the objective of intimidating Black and brown women into silence, pressuring us into

---

2   A term created by Moya Bailey to describe misogyny directed towards Black women, where race and gender both play roles in bias.

removing our voices from public discourse. On principle I refuse to let racists and misogynists stop me. I write and speak with the goal of improving the world for women of colour, all the Black and brown girls who will come after me into feminist spaces, in whatever way I can. That being said, receiving abuse online does have a personal cost. And then there are the hesitations that are part and parcel of growing up Black and female in this society.

Imposter syndrome struck so heavily that even with my MLitt in Gender Studies and a lifetime of experience as a Black woman, I spent the first few months wondering if I was a fraud. Still, the invitations came in steadily. I began to speak at feminist conferences and run workshops for women alongside my writing, bring conversations about Black feminism that were happening online into more physical spaces too. I have been Sister Outrider for a year and a half now, and at some point the balance shifted – my voice began to feel legitimate as I saw my writing make a difference. That name was a mantle I first adopted to give myself a confidence then lacking, a way of paying homage to my Black lesbian feminist foremother Audre Lorde. The persona of Sister Outrider – her ideas, the way she expresses them, what she makes possible – are all my work.

Digital space makes finding and connecting with other Black women in different locations possible. It facilitates powerful work that has impact in our lives offline as well as on. Black feminism is often perceived as Americentric, something many of us in the UK try to resist. Even in Britain, there's an idea that most of it happens in London – and while wonderful things are achieved in the south, that doesn't detract from the significance of Black feminism in other areas, including the north. The internet enables what geography hinders. It gives us the means to join the dots and build a more complete picture.

Through the internet, I have found my voice and carved my own niche in the global nexus of Black feminism. Claiming this place online has also allowed me to grow comfortable in my own skin, appreciate my skills, and find fulfilment in my work. Being witness to and part of this phenomenon has even shaped my research project as a PhD candidate. As well as influencing the lives of the women around me, the women who access my writing, being Sister Outrider has changed my own life. Writing online built a path I wasn't sure existed.

LAMENT: LIVING WITH THE CONSEQUENCES OF CONTRACEPTION

Jen McGregor

Dear D,

I miss you. That's probably hard to believe, considering how things ended between us, but... I do.

I know I shouldn't be writing this. It's been nearly ten years. I'm in my mid-30s. I'm settled, I'm happy, I've got what I always wanted. So I should have forgotten you long ago, right? I *should*.

I should...

* * *

I don't remember the exact date when I started getting Depo-Provera injections, but it was some time in September 2001. I was 18 years old and very proud of the amount of research I'd done into the different forms of contraception available to me. I think I must have had every leaflet, pamphlet and print-out in circulation at the time. I had read them all so many times that I'd practically memorised them. By the time I walked into the old Caledonia Youth clinic on Castle Terrace in Edinburgh, I felt ready to make my choice.

My excessive preparation wasn't just a hangover from studying or the result of being raised by a nurse. It was important to me to get this right, to know that when I began having penetrative sex I could reasonably expect that I wouldn't get pregnant.

The option I really preferred was sterilisation, which wasn't available to me and wouldn't become available until I reached my 30s. I was quite annoyed about this. I knew I didn't want children, and I reasoned that if I was old enough to become a parent then I was old enough to choose *not* to become one. I made that argument to various GPs on an annual basis until I turned 31. 'If I'd had a child the year I started menstruating,' I said to the doctor, 'that child would turn 16 this year. I would have been responsible for another human life for 16 years. It would be my responsibility to advise that child about sex and contraception. Are you really going to tell me that I've been old enough to be a parent for that long, but I'm *still* not old enough to make decisions about my own body?'

The doctor took my point.

★ ★ ★

It's ridiculous to long for you when I think about what you did to me. You broke my heart and several of my bones. Shall I give you the full list? My coccyx, my sacrum, my pelvis (in five different places), one of my lumbar vertebrae, a couple of toes and my scaphoid. (It's a small bone in the wrist. That one hurt more than all the others put together.)

Every single one of those fractures is a reason why I should never want you back in my life, and yet I do. I know this. The fact that I can't quash these feelings easily and completely is something I find confusing, upsetting and downright infuriating. You should be nothing more than an almost-forgotten memory of my younger, more experimental days.

I suppose it's not you I miss so much as the things you represent. When I was fearful, you were reassuring. When I was sick, you made me feel better. And when I was living under constraints I hadn't even begun to understand yet... you were freedom. I miss that freedom so much it hurts, and I doubt I'll ever find it again.

★ ★ ★

During my initial appointment at Caledonia Youth, the duty nurse talked me through my options. I explained my extensive reading and that I knew what I wanted, but she still ran through the list of alternatives.

Did I know about condoms? Of course I did, and of course I planned to use them for STD prevention, but I wanted a longer-term hormonal contraceptive to protect me against pregnancy. Had I considered the pill? I had, but I didn't trust myself to remember to take it at the same time each day. The patch? Again, I had, but I used to swim a lot and while the patch is meant to stay on in water I didn't want to take any chances. The IUS and IUD weren't recommended for a young woman who had never given birth (and I'd previously been advised not to use them due to the particular shape of my womb). The implant wasn't an option due to my lifelong horror of things under my skin (one of the many reasons for my desire to avoid pregnancy). I wanted the injection. The nurse booked me an appointment to come back and have it done.

* * *

I knew from the start that I couldn't have you forever. If truth be told, I didn't want to – I had a long-term plan and you weren't part of it. I wanted the kind of permanence you couldn't offer. But at 18 I thought that you and I suited each other well, and that was all I was looking for.

I loved that you weren't a massive commitment. You didn't demand my direct attention every single day the way some of the others did. We would reconnect every few months, one sharp and bitter-sweet meeting, then I'd carry something of you with me until the next time. That was all it took. All we needed. You were always there in the background, and that was exactly what I wanted.

With you in my life, all the gut-churning pain of my teenage years faded. I hadn't ever realised the extent of my misery until you released me from it. In exchange you took my ability to feel truly happy from me, but that seemed fair enough. I understood that this was the price and paid it gladly.

I didn't know about the secret, sneaky additional toll that you would exact until it was far too late. I didn't realise that you were sapping my youth and strength

**from me until I was past the point where the damage
could be undone. You betrayed me, and the worst
thing is that you didn't even need to because if you'd
made it clear to me that *that* was part of the price,
I would have agreed to it with barely a moment's
pause. I don't think you realised how
desperate that poor, sick girl was.**

* * *

My first few months on Depo were incredible. Not only did it
keep me pregnancy-free, the injection also liberated me from
the menstrual cycle that had been making my life hell since my
early teens. I had known that this was a possibility, but I hadn't
dared to hope that it might happen to me.

I loathed my periods from the first one onwards. My teens
were a seemingly endless cycle of mood swings, pain, nausea,
anaemia and feeling like a walking biohazard. I never settled into
any kind of useful pattern – my periods came six days apart, six
weeks apart or anything in between. They might last for a week,
they might last for three. My longest spell of uninterrupted
bleeding was 22 days. For most of that time I was using tampons
for the heaviest of flows, changing them hourly and still having
to change pads every few hours. It's hardly surprising that I was
horribly anaemic and fainting all over the place, or that I felt
too sick to eat much of the time, or that I was experiencing
cramps that left me doubled over and crying with pain.

Now, suddenly, all of that was over. I didn't know whether
the effect would be temporary or permanent, but I knew that I
loved it. I could leave the house without worrying that I would
start bleeding unexpectedly while I was out! I no longer found
myself in tears without any particular stimulus! I wasn't losing

several days a month to intolerable pain any more! The joy of sex was nothing compared the sheer delight of being set free from the misery of menstruation.

It would be another few months before Depo would start to affect my mood, so I had a little while to enjoy my euphoria before my ability to perceive such highs began to fade.

The first sign of trouble came after I'd been on Depo for a few years. I had been advised to come off it for a little while, just to give my body a break and to find out whether my menstrual cycle had ever settled down. This seemed like a good idea, so I decided to stop my injections for a year. My fear of pregnancy was undiminished, so for that year I also gave up male sexual partners, just to be on the safe side.

Twelve months and a couple of same-sex dalliances later, I still hadn't had a period. I realised that I ought to be concerned about this, but the next nurse I saw didn't seem too perturbed and I wasn't exactly keen for my cycle to resume, so I went back to having my injections as planned.

It wasn't until I was 25 and hadn't had a period in nearly seven years that the consequences became clear. My GP, realising that I'd been on Depo for most of that time, sent me for a bone density scan. I wasn't sure why, because loss of bone density wasn't a side-effect that had been mentioned in the literature I'd been given back when I was 18 and did all my research, so I went home and looked up more recent information. Sure enough, evidence had emerged that women who are on Depo long-term sometimes experience reduced bone density. And sure enough, I was one of those women. After the scan I was diagnosed with osteopenia, just above the borderline for osteoporosis. I was told to stop the injections at once. I did.

★ ★ ★

The day I learned of your betrayal... well, it wasn't entirely a surprise. My suspicions had been growing for a while. We had been together for too long, and I knew deep down that there was no way it could last – so if we were still going, as we were, then disaster must be lying in wait.

Yet even though it wasn't surprising, it was painful. I still liked what we had, I still loved the way you could set me free. I was 25 and there were things I wanted to be doing with my life, a career to build and my way to make. The last thing I wanted was to find myself abandoned by you. The freedom to explore other options was no freedom at all when I already knew that none of those options were what I wanted.

I suppose it's not fair to say you abandoned me. You didn't, really. I was the one who gave you up. But you were the one who left me no choice. When you're surrounded by medical staff outlining the dire consequences that await if you don't give up what you're doing, you should really listen. I didn't want to. But I did.

★ ★ ★

At that point I wasn't too concerned about my options. I had been told to switch to the pill, not just for contraception but also to combat the osteopenia. The pill would boost my oestrogen levels, I would follow a high calcium diet, and while I would always have low bone density for my age, at least the worst of the damage could be controlled. By the time I hit menopause, the doctors assured me, I would be back on track. Great.

I learned the hard way that I can't take oestrogen. The pill and the patch made me crazy – not in the catatonic, depressive way that I'd dealt with all my life, but in a way that felt really dangerous. I was constantly angry, bordering on violent, and I began to fear that I would hurt someone if I didn't stop the oestrogen. It became clear that I would have to manage the effects of the osteoporosis without it (which most likely means that by the time I hit menopause, my bones are going to be a series of holes held together by sheer bloody-mindedness).

But while I couldn't rely on the pill or the patch for bone density management, that wasn't my only concern. I was in a long-term relationship by this point and needed a reliable means of contraception. I talked my way into getting a copper coil, in spite of my oddly-shaped womb. I nearly threw up due to the pain of insertion, then bled heavily for six weeks straight before giving up and having it removed. Eventually I got a Mirena coil instead. It gave me constant mild nausea, low moods and a feeling of having a stone in my abdomen for a few years... but at least it kept my periods light and infrequent, and I was still free from the threat of pregnancy.

At long last, at the age of 31 and after several fractured bones due to the Depo side-effects, I was finally taken seriously and referred for sterilisation. The IUD would be taken out in the same operation, and pregnancy would be off the table forever. My relief was palpable.

After so much opposition, I was anticipating problems all the way up to the moment when I felt the anaesthetic chilling the veins in the back of my hand. The hospital staff who prepared me for the operation asked me again and again to confirm the procedure I was having, to confirm that I knew it was permanent and potentially irreversible. I answered over and over again, eager to prove that yes, yes, I knew exactly what I was doing and that after so many years of fighting for my

Filshie clips I was never going to part company with them ever. I understood why they had to ask, and why they had to do it repeatedly. I didn't mind that.

What I *did* mind was the moment when one nurse asked me 'Is your husband happy for you to have this procedure?'

Er, what? I remember thinking. *It's 2014, I'm an adult, my husband doesn't get to tell me what I can and can't do with my body.* I replied politely that he was indeed, and that if they needed confirmation then they would find him in the waiting room and could ask him themselves. They didn't.

I told my husband about that question afterwards. He seemed quite annoyed at the idea that I should require either his permission or his blessing, considering that it's my body and not his. It was the response I expected, and I wouldn't have married anyone who might have replied differently. After all, it's the hospital's job to tend to my health, not my marriage.

* * *

I'm not coming back, of course. I can't. I know all too well what the consequences would be, and putting myself back on that path to self-destruction would be unfair to me and everyone who cares about me. I'm old enough and experienced enough to know that you would probably make good on your threat to break my spine eventually.

But I would be lying if I said I'm not tempted. There are times, mostly when it's late at night and I'm sick with pain and rage, when the feeling of you haunting my thoughts and my body is all but unbearable. I hate you and miss you and hate you and miss you

and in those moments I entertain mad fantasies of fleeing it all and coming straight back to you.

How long would it last? I don't know. A year, perhaps. Two if I'm lucky and very careful. But what a year it might be...

I hate you more for leaving me to live with this temptation than for hurting me in the first place.

★ ★ ★

It's now just over two years since I got sterilised. Two years with no hormonal contraception. After the initial bleeding that followed the removal of the IUD, it took several months for my menstrual cycle to show up again. I've been having reasonably regular periods for just over a year... but these past few months, they've started to get less regular, heavier and more painful. Two months ago, for the first time in years, I experienced such intense nausea and cramp that I couldn't eat or stand up. As I write this, I am terrified that I'm going to lose my health to my menstrual cycle again and that this time there will be nothing I can do about it.

I've just turned 34 and I'm extremely concerned about how the menopause is going to affect me. As my bones crumble, how fragile will I become? Will I have to spend my life doing everything with exceptional caution, never running or jumping or climbing or dancing in case I break something? I've broken bones in my spine before, what if the next fracture is the one that robs me of my ability to walk? How far will I get before that happens, before I lose my ability to live independently? Or will continue to be lucky and only break less important bones?

I feel like I've paid a hefty price for the years I spent on Depo, for wanting to control my sex life and my menstruation. To solve one set of health problems, I inadvertently created another. I didn't realise, back when I embarked on this journey at the age of 18, just how far contraception and women's health still have to go. I learned that one the hard way. Whether that's the result of institutional sexism in the medical profession or simply a matter of where we are in the timeline of medical developments may be debatable, but the fact remains that there are plenty of women out there in my situation, with messy and uncontrollable bodies and situations, for whom 'woman' feels more like a diagnosis than a sex category. What's to be done about us? I don't know. Probably nothing that will happen in time for my generation. But I fervently hope that for future teenagers exploring their options, there will be forms of contraception that allow them to have their bodily autonomy *and* their health – the truest form of sexual equality I can imagine.

★ ★ ★

Depo, I loved you.

I wish you had loved me.

– Jen

THESE SHADOWS, THESE GHOSTS

Laura Lam

'*Ghost, n.* The outward and visible sign of an inward fear.'
– Ambrose Bierce

Content note: This essay mentions rape, domestic abuse, and gun violence.

My mother and I grew up under the shadows of nasty women
– the previous two generations of the Baxter family. I can't
remember when I first started learning bits of their stories from
my mother – a detail here, a hint there. The stories were more
about my grandmother than my great-grandmother, at first. I
only knew my grandmother had done something terrible by
the way the shadows would play over my mother's face when
I asked about her. Learning about my great-grandmother was
easier. My mother had hazy memories and passed down recol-
lections. Yet I was still so curious about the other Baxter woman.
More clues, more particulars, and gradually the puzzle pieces
fell into place. One sunny day after flute rehearsal, I guessed
what my grandmother had done.

The stories of these two complicated, flawed, beautiful and
nasty women have haunted me and my mother throughout
our lives. Echoes of them have appeared in my fiction, hidden
glimpses of who I think they might have been. Now, both my
mother and I are going to exorcise those ghosts – searching for
more answers, writing them down, bringing them back to life.

Many of the minutiae of my great-grandmother's life have
been lost to time, much as we're trying to find out more. Her
name had been Sarah, and she'd married my great-grandfather
just after World War One. She'd come from abject poverty: her

parents had given her to an orphanage because they couldn't afford to feed her. Her new husband was a rich playboy, but we're not sure how he made his fortune. Property or lumber, maybe, or older money passed down and keenly invested. Almost all of the wealth was lost in the Great Depression. Because Sarah's husband had inherited the money, he didn't know how to build it back up. The loss crushed him and he turned to drink. Sarah kept some of her jewels, slowly pawning them to help her and her daughters, Barbara and Jean, get by. She hid the jewels in her Kotex box. One day, her husband found them. Sarah knew he would drink all their money away, so she shot him in the leg. We don't know if this happened during the dramatic moment of discovery, if she'd had the gun already or bought one later, but she pulled the trigger on him at some point. She kicked him out and he limped off, evidently becoming a hobo who rode the rails.

Sarah, now a single mother in the 1930s, picked herself back up. She became a buyer for Macy's in a time when women rarely worked and provided for herself and her children. She worked for Macy's until the late 1950s when she married her second husband, Carl, a man who owned a successful brewery. So, she became financially comfortable again and took no nonsense from anyone.

Inspiring as the bare bones are, Sarah was not an uncomplicated hero. My mother remembers her own grandmother as cold and almost cruel. She was not a warm and caring parent to my grandmother. Barbara had to make her bed so tightly that Sarah could bounce a quarter off of it. She'd go around the house with white gloves, admonishing her daughters if, after running a fingertip along the mantelpiece, it came away grey with dust. Sarah was hard, exacting, but it might have been because she wanted to guide Barbara into a life easier than her own. A life of running a household and not having to be a working mother. This didn't exactly go to plan.

In the late 1940s, my grandmother was a model. Glamourous

and gorgeous, she helped introduce the colours kelly green and navy blue on the runway. Her career only grew, but then she was horribly attacked and raped by a photographer. We're unsure if they were dating or not. She became pregnant. A few months later, he attacked her again so violently she lost the baby. Soon after, she met my grandfather: tall, dark-haired, and handsome in a nerdy, poindexter sort of way. He was brilliant, held an electrical engineering doctorate and worked with computers back when they were the size of rooms. He was not violent. He seemed safe. She married him almost immediately, giving up the runway and the limelight. She settled into the role of the 1950s housewife. It was a mould she would never fit.

Barbara found out her husband had kept secrets from her. He didn't have much choice in the matter. The CIA had paid for his PhD; Barbara knew that, but she was not immediately aware he was an operative during his many overseas visits. My mother and I are in the process of collecting the data needed for a Freedom of Information Request to see if we can obtain more details about what he actually did, though we suspect it may still be classified. My mother knows he went behind the Iron Curtain with a fake name and a cyanide pill, doing some type of computer and surveillance work.

Barbara's life as a housewife was not filled with as many thrills as when she was a model. She had three children: in 1950, not long after her marriage, my mother in 1953, and her little sister in 1960. It was after the third pregnancy that my grandmother's mental health took a huge downturn. She retreated to her room for three months when they moved from outside Washington, D.C. to Los Angeles. She might have found out what her husband truly did around this time. Though in need of mental health support, she never received any for her rape, her PTSD, or her three bouts of worsening post-natal depression.

My grandmother tried to throw herself into the homemaker role, becoming a Girl Scout leader and also doing art in her spare time to give her a little freedom. By the time she'd had her third child, my aunt, she was fully paranoid schizophrenic. When out driving, my grandmother would sometimes pull over, hissing at her children to duck down because the kangaroomen and the zookeepers were after them. Agents of my grandfather, presumably, keeping an eye on her.

My mother's childhood was filled with violence and fear. She never knew from one minute to the next if an innocent comment would set her mother off and either she or one of her sisters would be dragged down the hall by their hair or given a black eye or a fat lip. Her father never protected his children from their mother. He turned a blind eye to it and escaped into his world of numbers, equations, and the secrets of his work, first at the CIA and later at Aerospace Corporation. My mother reacted to this violence by trying to become invisible. However, her childhood was not all horrible. She roamed the fields and tide pools of San Pedro to stay out of the house and away from her mother. She had many pets: a dog, a cat, chickens, a pigeon, hamsters, and a horse. Galloping her horse at full speed and screaming at the top of her lungs helped her feel free, at least for a while.

My grandmother's mental health worsened. The child abuse grew more severe. Her art grew stranger. When I was three, my grandmother had lung cancer from years of smoking. My mother, then six months pregnant with my little brother, flew out to the East Coast with me as fast as she could, but Barbara died twenty minutes before we reached the hospital. While we were back East, we stayed with my youngest aunt and went to my grandmother's apartment. In the entry hall was a ceramic cauliflower-like sculpture with disembodied doll parts glued all over it, with other limbs and heads embedded, as though struggling to escape. It was titled 'mother.' I screamed when I saw it and they had to cover it with a sheet.

My grandfather never helped his wife get treatment due to the stigma of mental health at the time. It ended up costing him dearly. My grandparents divorced when my mother was fifteen. My mother had to tell the judge she and her younger sister would rather live with their father. For three years, my grandparents were separated and dated other people. My grandmother chose increasingly strange men, including one who shot and killed my mother's dog when she was away for her first year of college. When my mother was eighteen and her father decided to properly divorce his wife to marry his new girlfriend, Barbara bought a gun, legally, and shot him. She paused to reload, and shot him a few more times. My mother was eighteen, just starting her second year of college.

The courtroom of the trial for first degree murder is one of the few times all three Baxter women were together. Sarah pale and disapproving. Barbara sitting at the defence table, her gaze vague. Sally, my mother, taking the stand to testify against her own mother. Barbara was sent to a mental health facility instead of prison, finally getting care. We're unsure how good the care actually was in that 1970s institution, but she became more stable and was released, though my mother and grandmother had an understandably strained relationship afterwards.

My mother coped as best as she could, moving north from Los Angeles to San Francisco and doing something called Primal Therapy. Some of her father's inheritance paid for her school. She lived her own life, not without its own plot twists and difficulties, and became a model like her mother. She floated about in other jobs like running an ill-fated sign business with my father, which swallowed the last of her inheritance. After my parents divorced, she went back to university for her Master's degree. For a long time, she didn't want children, terrified they might feel about her the way she felt about her own mother. Eventually she had me and my brother, but she followed her own intuition about how to be a parent, mostly by doing the opposite of what her parents did.

Sometimes, growing up, I felt like the Baxter women were cursed. They were put in difficult situations, and my grandmother especially could have lived such a different life had she received less cruelty and more care. In a flat re-telling, these women could have been cast as villains. The newspaper articles about my grandmother around the trial certainly did – they called her a 'red-headed devil' and a 'murderess'.

The curse broke with me. My childhood was happy – not perfectly stable – but full of love and warmth. And from that distance of comfort, it made the lives of my grandmother and her mother all the more jarring to me. Paranoid schizophrenia can often skip generations, and usually manifests when someone is in their teens or thirties. As a teen, that anxiety niggled at me, and I wondered if I'd hallucinate, seeing my own versions of kangaroomen and zookeepers. Instead, I navigated various other mental health issues – severe anxiety, an eating disorder, and depression. But my mother made sure I had help and support, and as an adult nearing thirty, my mental health is managed well. My life is not as interesting as the other women in my family, and I'm fully fine with that.

I didn't want to see their stories disappear. In my undergraduate degree, I wrote a short story inspired by Sarah, and it saw one of my early publications in my university literary journal. I moved into science fiction and fantasy, which is where I've built my career since 2012.

Last year, my mother and I decided we would collaborate on a book about our family in a braided narrative of three generations. Their stories echoed each other in strange parallels. All three time periods deal with the threat or aftermath of war: the brief respite between WWI and WWII, the end of WWII, and the Vietnam War for my mother's time as a hippie in the 1970s. There is the recurring motif of the gun through two narratives. There are breakdowns of relationships, with men looking the other way when times grew difficult, and a focus on motherhood and mental health. Wealth was gained and lost. My mother is going to write her own story, we're both going to write Barbara's, and I'll take the bulk of Sarah's, which requires the heaviest fictional veneer. It'll be a book of tragic, strong women. We've started gathering information and outlining, and my mother went over this very essay, adding detail and weaving in her own lived experience.

The echoes of the Baxter women I never knew shaped the woman I am today. Their stories resulted in my mother being a staunch feminist, and raising me from a young age to think that I can do whatever I put my mind to and that there are no limits. Two years ago, I wrote a short story for another feminist anthology – *Cranky Ladies of History*. In that collection, writers wrote about women who bucked the trend of history. I wrote about Jeanne de Clisson, The Lioness of Brittany, a pirate in the 1300s who personally beheaded noblemen with an axe to avenge the death of her husband.

Women who make themselves heard have insults flung at them by those threatened by a change in the status quo. My mother and I both voted for a certain nasty woman in the 2016 US presidential election. Go back another generation or two and my grandmother and great-grandmother would be labelled witches or traitors to their assumed gender roles. Even after my great-grandmother clawed her way back into wealth for the second time, she had straddled the divide between classes too often to ever be at home in either world. My grandmother couldn't be Susie Homemaker, and my mother refused to let her past define her future.

My mother and I are working together, delving through the past, finding out what we can and making up the rest. One of the book's themes is the notion of sins being revisited down through the next generation, and how breaking that cycle is difficult but possible. We'll be bringing these nasty women back to life, at least for the length of a book. Women can change their own narrative. We can cry out, speak loudly, hold our chin up. Yes, we might be called names. We might be pushed back. But we'll still cry out and make ourselves heard.

THE NASTINESS OF SURVIVAL

Mel Reeve

Content note: This essay mentions some descriptive examples of sexual violence and recovery.

I am a survivor of rape and emotional abuse, but I do not fit into the 'right' definition of someone who has been raped. I was drunk, I told him I loved him, I hid my tears, I told him it was okay afterwards, I didn't call the police, I tried to pretend I was okay and I told my friends and family it was okay. Now that I am free from him and starting to understand my pain, I refuse to be hurt in a way that is easy to look at for the convenience of others.

I am not beautiful, quiet and devastated in my pain like a heroine in a Shakespearean drama; I am no Ophelia quietly lying down in the river with my pain, there is no bravery or greater symbolism to the hardships I experience. My existence as a survivor is inconvenient at best and a constant act of defiance at worst because I reject the two choices I am given by society; the 'perfect survivor' and the 'bad survivor'. Neither choice is real although it is instilled in us from an early age that they are, but it is useful to apply these labels as a way to describe this dichotomy. The term 'victim' is not one I apply to myself, as many other survivors of sexual assault do not. We see ourselves and choose to describe ourselves as survivors.

The ideal of a 'perfect survivor' goes something like this: a woman is attacked by a masked man in an alley, she calls the police immediately, cries just the right amount before healing bravely and getting on with her life. This may be someone's story and it is just as valid as any other, but it is not the only way to be a survivor and it is certainly not the 'right' way to be raped. There is no 'right' way, which means there is no right way to go on living afterwards. The only thing you have to do to be a survivor is to be raped and then survive.

The reality of my experiences is that they are complicated and do not fit society's construction of how someone who has been raped should behave, which means I cannot be the 'good' survivor and must become the opposite – the 'bad survivor'. This identity which is forced onto us is the harsh reality of surviving rape and abuse; we are expected to be above reproach, to have followed a specific set of rules and experiences otherwise what happened to us is deemed invalid.

I didn't even know I'd been raped for a while. This is part of what makes me a bad survivor. How can something that life-changing happen without you even knowing? I knew on some level that something very wrong had happened to me. I knew that when a friend told me about her experiences at the hands of a man who purported to love her that something inside me heard and reflected her pain on a level deeper than simple empathy, but I hid it from myself and everyone else. My life fractured and crumbled around me while I struggled to hold my head up above the rubble and say 'this is okay'.

Rape turned me into a good liar. That is the most dangerous truth because we are so afraid of this fake 'bad survivor' who invents her pain to punish men. She does not exist. What happened to me is no less real because I hid it. I told my mother, I told my friends, I told my doctor, I told him and I told myself that nothing had happened to me really, or that if it had happened to me then there were reasons and excuses which made it something else. It's hard to admit because the world expects a rape survivor to be the most honest; no short skirts or alcohol, not at the hands of your boyfriend, and certainly not someone you have defended in the past. We are asked to prove what happened to us in order to reassure people that we are not like 'those' women, the liars who throw wild accusations and want to destroy the lives of poor innocent men who have done nothing. 'Those' nasty, dishonest women who, of course, do not actually exist.

My personal experiences of openly declaring myself a survivor taught me that if you want to tell someone that their friend or acquaintance raped you, you must be prepared for an intense examination of your every mistake, accidental dishonesty or white lie. If they can find anything (which they will, because we are human) it may well be enough for them to discredit you in their own minds, because that is easier than accepting rapists live among us. They are not scary monsters hiding in the dark, they are part of our society, our colleagues and our friends.

If we acknowledge that these two concepts, the 'perfect survivor' and the 'bad survivor' do not exist, and that it is far more likely to be your friend, boyfriend, girlfriend or lover who harms, rather than masked men in alleys, then we can no longer expect survivors to contextualise what happened for other people's comfort. We must instead acknowledge the reality of what happens. Unfortunately, this isn't the empowering and righteous process it might sound. It's unpleasant and it can make you nasty.

After I started to talk about what happened to me, I became perceived as objectionable. Difficult. I chose to share what happened to me with a few friends who then chose to ignore the facts of what my abuser did. I was not the perfect survivor, which to them meant I must be the other option – a liar. They enabled my abuser by tacit approval of his actions, which was possible because his particular nastiness was kept hidden while I wore mine proudly and honestly.

This is why it's so important to me not to sugar-coat my experiences, to speak honestly about how I am a survivor of rape and abuse and still a human being, and of the choices I made to survive and how hard it is to exist afterwards. If we tear down this ideal of what a survivor of rape should be and how they should cope, I can only hope it will become harder for those who excuse rapists and abusers because the truth is too inconvenient, and that makes me feel a step closer to holding my rapist to account.

I also want to acknowledge that my survival is not a noble struggle that has shaped me, it is not a story of redemption or overcoming my inner demons; I can be cruel to the people I love. I do not trust people until they have proven themselves over and over to me. Worst of all, sometimes I cannot be there for the people I love when they are in pain because, in that moment, the pain I carry is the worst pain in the world. I have been forced to live with something awful, and I will never be grateful for the personal development I have had to endure to survive it.

Acknowledging that I did things I am not proud of while being abused has been a big part of my survival. Thanks to the incredible support of Rape Crisis Glasgow, I know now that this is quite a common response to trauma. When we are in situations of high stress, particularly those that push us into survival mode, we make decisions that we think, on an instinctual level, will help us to survive. We feel how a caveman would when faced with a sabre-tooth tiger, even if the danger is more psychological or complex than a tiger bite. When we calm down or are able to escape this situation we may find that this decision does not fit with our morals and feelings as we would normally relate to the world. This is conceptualised in a popular theory used to understand trauma called the 'Window of Tolerance', coined by Dr. Dan Siegel.

Recently, I read an article which cited several rape cases found in the news, and it proposed rapists don't know they are rapists. When I'd finished this article I closed my browser window and

I sat silently for a few moments. I wanted to cry, I wanted to scream and yell and fall apart because this is the most dangerous myth of all – that our assailants are not dangerous people. These people who are capable of such intentional, awful violation and manipulation, well, they just don't *know* what they are doing. It's an accident, a consequence of miscommunication, a terrible mistake.

Rapists know they are rapists. Our laws and the way we speak about these topics lend silent approval to their behaviour and allow them to commit sexual assault and abuse and declare themselves feminists in the same day. This begins with the kind of consent education which declares consent to be 'sexy' rather than a fundamental, essential element of what makes it sex rather than rape, and ends with the fact that the law is essentially useless to most survivors and we know that so deeply most of us don't even have the chance to try.

The narrative around consent, assault and the innate nastiness of abuse and surviving abuse is presented in some circles as a problem that can be fixed by consent education, with slogans like 'consent is sexy!' and cute stickers that declare the wearer to be super keen on consent. I am here to propose that this doesn't help. I think consent education is important in terms of teaching young people that their bodies do not belong to anyone, that they can say no whenever they want to, and what options are available if someone violates that. I think it is also important that we instil the strongest possible sense of shame into young rapists and potential rapists. But I don't believe that this endemic problem is solvable by polite conversations and structured lessons because that feeds into the myth that rape is an accident caused by miscommunication rather than a conscious, violent and devastating choice.

I have lost friends and had terrible arguments with family because of what happened to me. I don't know how to be any other way than the person I am and the person I am is in spite of what happened, but the consequences are the same regardless of the why. My rape has shaped me and I have no way to stay quiet about it. I spent too long having my voice silenced.

Not every survivor feels able to talk about what happened to them and I am no braver or stronger because I can talk about it. I am the kind of person who always discussed the big things in my life, good or bad, and surviving the terrible things that happened to me is woven into every day of my life, sometimes in obvious ways and sometimes in small, barely perceptible ones. I used to dream of revenge, of staring my abuser in the face and asking him to declare in front of a room full of people that he knows what he did. Accepting that I will probably never get the opportunity to be a righteously angry witness in front of those that still support and believe him comes with accepting that he knows what he did. I have to accept that his actions were conscious decisions made with either no regard for the consequences, or that the consequences were his intention. Either way, I can't go back. I have to live with this, so I might as well make it my own.

If you are reading this as a survivor, I don't presume to know your situation or that I have an answer for how to get through this terrible thing we have known, but I would suggest that if you haven't already, try to see your nastiness as a part of your whole. Particularly for women, who are taught to be quiet, unobjectionable; we are sugar and spice and pleasant and helpful – and this contributes to the silence, the polite, dreadful silence that overcomes us when we try to talk about what happened.

I know it is impolite to talk about the time my humanity was stripped from me and I was treated like an object to be used. It is not at all acceptable to say I know how it feels to look the man that is supposed to love me in the eye and understand that he has so little regard for me that he could do anything to me and we both know nothing will ever happen to him. I understand that is not an easy or nice thing to hear. It is not an easy thing for me to write. It is even less easy for me to live with. But I do.

That is why I am proudly and vocally a nasty woman; tired of making excuses, of letting politeness stop me from defending myself. I lost too much when I was silent, nice and accommodating and I met someone who chose to take advantage of that. It's too late to stop what happened to me but the more I verbalise it, the more I force the discomfort of my existence into society – in refusing to conform to the ideal of the 'perfect survivor' whilst also refusing to ignore what happened – the better it seems to be for me.

I shout about what happened to me in my poetry and in essays like this. I tell anecdotes about the darkest moments of my life as jokes and I try my best to stare my abuser in the eye when the pain becomes too much, rather than let him continue to own me through my past. Some people have said that it saddens them to see me define myself as a victim (which I do not) and that I *can* go back to being the person I was before. I can't. The awfulness of what happened to me has taken something away which I cannot get back. I have a choice between keeping this enormous pain in my head or expelling it out into the world as my only route to hold him to account, and to offer it as a form of protection or comfort for those who have experienced what I have.

I invite you all to look at my pain, to be uncomfortable when I talk about the worst of humanity – the worst of the people in your social circles and your workplace – and how we cannot fix this with polite lessons or twee stickers, forgiveness or apologies. I speak openly about how unkind my trauma makes me. Ceasing to be nice and choosing to instead be a little nasty does not mean I cease to exist and I think that is a victory of some kind.

AGAINST STEREOTYPES: WORKING CLASS GIRLS AND WORKING CLASS ART

Laura Waddell

There are few stories told about working class girls, whether the thinness of stereotype, or typeset in books.

There was a chemist on the main street of the post-industrial town I grew up in, and it stocked makeup products accessible to the slim pocket money jangling in my butterfly-embroidered purse. The brand names were unheard of; their coyly sensual, vaguely European sounding language riffing off their better known counterparts and emblazoning dusty, battered boxes of powders and lotions in fonts with flourishes.

It was the late 90s, but knock-off products take a while to catch up, and there was an 80s feel about much of the pastel, gauzy packaging with its lush, womanly florals. I'd take my time whilst other customers came and went, distantly ringing the bell over the door at the other end of the long narrow shop, seeking out the most garish and youthful items among the shelves. I distinctly remember chemical-cherry scented, opaque red lip gloss, dispensed from a rollerball in a glass tube, and the feel of applying it, round and round. It was vulgarly thick and shiny, with all the subtlety of neon, and to me it was perfect. Nothing has better fitted the word 'gloopy'; it sat on top of my petted teenage lips like a coat of bulky varnish, as sticky as sweet and sour sauce, and as cloying.

Cherries appeared to be sexual in a way I did not understand, only that their image was some semiotic wink to coquettish adult fun, and association with them, or at least, the lab-approximation synthetic scent and exaggerated illustration of my lip gloss, felt safely bold. I wore the stuff slopped on in plump layers, habitually tasting it with the tip of my tongue, necessitating performative reapplication. The unnatural cherry did not, unfortunately, extend to flavour. Once I wrote my name with it, rolling out wet letters one by one in one of the many notebooks I'd carry around to fill between lessons with poetry and quotes, only for the pages to smear, stick together, and tear.

Testing the self in any number of possible incarnations at such a formative age depends upon what's available to strike against to see sparks. Fantasies form guided by frames of inspiration and example, and experiments are conducted to the extent of tangible means.

What are the models and stereotypes attached to teenage girls, and especially those, like me, from working class backgrounds? As is the nature of stereotype, they are often, where they exist at all, unkind and hollow. On the rota is the pony-obsessed girl with white ribbons in her horse's hair. A bit twee, nowadays, and a cliché definitely out of my price range. Boys of public consciousness get a wider array of sports to be mad about (most reliably, football), and for those at fancier schools than mine, rugby, polo, and cricket, or tennis with lemonade served by the side of the court. Honing in more closely on the socio-economic demographic I'm from, stereotypical boys get to run around freely on shadowy council estates, shaven headed and prone to petty, visceral violence, often in packs. Working class girls appear in the imagination only to push prams on a designated dotted mental line across these stark spaces already graffitied by the boys, having, according to tabloid convention, dropped out of school. What about the provocative St Trinian's type, from films I watched before old enough to find their sexualisation problematic, whose essential components of rule breaking and wildness, since modernised to gelled-hair, lip-smacking and piercings behind-the-bike-sheds on youth TV? We didn't have bike sheds, but maybe my cherry lip gloss and short skirts more or less fit that paper doll's dimensions, or were, at least, easily vamped up for torn-tights, unheimlich Hallowe'en costumes.

I have never, to deflate the image, chewed gum. Perhaps the moping bookish girl, existing primarily within the DVD jewel cases of American films, who'd inevitably take her glasses off, swapping books for some undeserving boy? I kept the books, and I kept my glasses on, wearing them with the lip gloss, and in my council estate flat bedroom which was a world away from Cadillacs and prom. The teenage boys of cliché-land are not often afforded the same transformation opportunities, or, for that matter, books.

Whilst girls are presented in a ditsy pink, perfumed haze of pubescent preening, teenage boys get to be disgusting, with comic depictions of trash-filled bedrooms and questionable hygiene, a precursor to patronising ideas of having to be looked after even as grown men, displayed in painfully unfunny 'wife's away' or 'what happens when Dad's in charge' memes which are as harmful to female domestic liberation as they are to conceptions of capable fatherhood.

But to anyone who ever was a teenage girl, we know we were just as vile. As much a part of my Proustian memory conjured by synthetic cherry is cherry Cola; miniature cans of which, bought from Woolworths, lay empty and scattered around my bedroom alongside grease-smeared pizza boxes shoved under a mattress with springs poking into my back, and no money to replace it. I had wind chimes suspended from the ceiling, but no wind, never caring to open my window to let in fresh air, and perched on stacks of books, dead plants - even withered cacti – I'd never watered. The peachy cleaning solution used to tend my just-pierced eleven year old ears smelt fresh, exciting, and clinical; the pile of T-shirts and knickers on the floor, and any other surface and the resented, crumpled PE kit certainly did not.

On frequent weekend sleepovers my pals and I were as likely to do each other's nails or dance around to Spice Girls tracks, mouthing all the words to B-sides ('Bumper to Bumper', baby), as we were to hibernate in a pile of quilts, junk-food, and general grime for 48 hours; surrogate siblings who'd bathe in mutual laziness and grot, surfacing only to rummage through kitchen cupboards and return, monosyllabically grunting, with sustenance. In our working class fridges and cupboards we'd find cheap, airy two litre tubs of ice cream, or supermarket own brand crisps, sliced so thinly as to be translucent at the edges. Without cable, we'd adjust long silver TV aerials to catch terrestrial signals, and ignore any sounds from neighbours or arguments with our own families through the thin walls, which were a sort of thickened cardboard in my house and too easy to accidentally punch a hole straight through in a fit of claustro-phobic adolescent emotion.

I suspect teenage stereotypes do not form a perfect fit in most cases; as a working class girl, they felt particularly cruel, narrow, and encroaching and I couldn't recognise much of myself in them.

Soon, I'd outgrown stereotypes available to me at all, with nothing, even, to simply clash or identify with. The first in my family, I was destined to go to university, achieving high grades and possessing a frenzied love for books that had emerged when I'd tell stories as a toddler, asking for them to be written down by patient adults, or when, at nursery, the teachers thought it odd I'd sit and look at books before I could read them and asked my mum if I could be encouraged to spend less time fasci-natedly flipping through pages. (She dismissed this.) Was such a draw to books a kind of escapism? A rebellion?

Over the years and tepid cups of tea therapists, engaged for depression, have asked me variations on this theme since. What about the hostile school environment? No, it was an innate love. 'Are you sure you want to study English literature?' a career advisor at high school asked, having a mandatory glance over the future plans of the class of 2004. Believing it to be kindness, I hope, she told me kids of my background usually got on better at technical college, studying something practical, with better prospects of employability. Arts were tricky; there would be loan debt. Most kids, she said, most working class kids, didn't go down that route. Feeling a burning desire to study what I've always deeply been drawn to, I ignored the worst advice I've ever been given, and followed my vocation. Most importantly of all, this route to be among books, and to study art, manifested itself because I was fortunate enough to be born at the right time to benefit from Scotland's free higher education policy, a chance and liberation that still moves me to tears whenever it arises in political debate.

But whilst the advice in that dimly lit school office was bad, one point was true. Working class kids do not enter careers in the arts or in media as frequently, or as comfortably, as their better off counterparts, and particularly in the field I'm now in, of publishing. It is not our stereotype, and it is not, for the most part, our reality.

College films focusing on the student experience are often Hollywood-created and so distanced regardless, but they do not tend to tell tales of hardship and struggle. Students walking across sunny, grassy lawns with books under arms or draping a varsity sweatshirt around a sweetheart's shoulders aren't usually heading to a fast food outlet to pick up an apron afterwards, or jumping on a bus home to a damp flat after a date.

In art and literary history, where there are tales of starving artists, they're typically male; Van Gogh's sparse bedroom, captured with its blue walls in his painting Bedroom in Aries; Rimbaud's runaway hustling, or the evocative hunger poetry of Jacques

Prevert, staring at unobtainable food with ravenous need. In the retelling, it's a bohemianism that is at times overly romanticised; stripped of its difficult details, reduced to noble macho suffering for the sake of greater things, for art. It's an aesthetic of its own; the fantasy built, and exploited by tedious poets or typewriter emblazoned T-shirt manufacturers.

So too, in diaries; we see male writers and journalists like Henry Miller document a writer's life waiting for the next pay cheque, but, given the even greater barriers to poor women in accessing artistic expression or to women throughout history more generally, struggling to see their art recognised and where recognised, taken seriously, there are far fewer documentations of poor women artists, few enough not to have penetrated public consciousness with their own stereotype. There is no real struggling female artist cliché in traditional or popular culture, and no examples of women writing from poverty have become canon, in part because the professionalisation of art shut out women of all social backgrounds for many years, not just poor ones, but reducing it to a hobbyist, crafting leisure activity for the well-off.

In the present day, cold hard cash is the still the obvious barrier to people of working class backgrounds accessing the arts. Entry costs to study aside, it's hard to forge a stable career in a sector increasingly low on funds. In this time of austerity and increasing government cuts, libraries are closing at a faster rate than ever before, hitting disadvantaged areas more strongly, environments where people cannot as easily afford to travel, or to buy books. Arts departments are having resources slashed, and arts journalism is in a fragile state, prone to the dual spectres of redundancy and non-specialist, aggregated content to pop out on rolling ticker feeds.

Working as an artist, of any sort, requires walking a financial tightrope. Costs to practise visual art, whether materials for sculptors or equipment for photographers, can be prohibitive.

A professional writer, a career with median income far below minimum wage, requires, if no independent wealth, a second, often full-time job. It is hard, and it is harder for those without additional means to fall back upon. Sometimes it is hard to just find the extra energy on top of other labour and financial stresses.

Coming from a background of lesser financial backing also has a psychological impact on entering a career in the arts with confidence. Walking into a classroom full of peers who've never had access restricted to books, museums, or galleries, who come from families with easy familiarity with higher education and the arts is daunting, when you are a working class child who has learned to savour the smallest, most limited access, and from a family who have never before been able to afford further study. Snobbery exists, of course, but it's also a matter of advance preparation and preliminary resources.

When my student loan first entered my bank balance, the green digits peered at through a grubby cash machine screen with awe, I went straight to a café on campus and in a fit of extravagance bought a large coffee, a pasty, and some overpriced, prepackaged fresh fruit glistening temptingly under cabinet lights. The world, it felt in that moment, perched on a bar stool biting into pineapple, was mine.

Later, I was struck by anxiety; how could I have spent what felt at the time like so much money on frivolity? And how stupid, I felt, self-protectively limiting, squeezing myself back into a more realistic, smaller mental shape, to be so excited by the moment of careless, sweet-tasting excess.

I used my library card well, but had never summered in France like many other students in the language module I tacked on to my first year course load. Parents of friends who'd given them glimpses into their own professional careers, arts or otherwise, seemed exotic, distant creatures – certainly no better or worse for it – but providers of alternate vision.

Although it is increasingly common, my grandmother then

and now still tells anyone – strangers, taxi drivers - that her granddaughter went to university. *It's not that rare for working class kids anymore,* I say. But to her generation, it's another world, and still a marvel, my passing through to undiscovered educational lands a totem.

There is a familiarity gap. At times, among middle class peers, I'd become aware of my lack of arts exposure, and occasionally have a mild crisis of confidence. Never ashamed of my background, or believing it made me any lesser, and determined to advocate for the importance of arts access to working class children, it was in early student years still a barrier to overcome, and an extra layer of fatigue.

Where are the role models and guides, and predecessors from our own families and communities? Where even, are our stereotypes? And where is the belief that working in the arts is possible and suitable for working class children, or that arts are important to access for working class adults? That arts are for the working class at all? The library I depended upon, as a child who was later to work in publishing, the library where I read every single children's book, voraciously checking out twelve at a time and racing through them, has since been closed by council cuts. Had this happened when I was a frequent user as a child, it would have had a devastating impact on me.

On a working trip last summer I was told by an author over a lunchtime glass of wine in London that I was one of only about ten working class people he'd met in the industry (of publishing/writing) in the last ten years. Even then, it only came up because we'd been talking about it, as it was the subject of his next book – he might not otherwise have known, he said, what my class was at all.

Wincing over the capital price of a second round at the bar, I wondered whether there are now more of us than might be perceived. It's more difficult for working class people to enter the arts, but it's also assumed the arts are not appreciated by us, and any interest revealed can occasionally lead to cases of mistaken middle class identity. The working class are not one monocultural block, but a lack of stories told from our perspective has lent itself to dull, flattened portrayals that do not reflect the diversity of reality.

The stereotypes of pastimes and tastes attached to class are plentiful and reductive, groaning through TV sets and passed around like germs in the playground. Before polling days politicians visit working class areas and stand, thickly, with a pint in hand, talking of simple desires and simple needs. Notably, they never stand with a book in hand talking of art and access, or reflect on the multi-faceted needs of working class people and impoverished communities.

Often, as a shallow vote grabber, attempts are made to polarise a liberal elite and ordinary working people, as though art and education is for one class, and gravy and labour the other. The language used is thick in allusion. Sometimes, this sticks. Despite a history of activism and creativity, the lack of working class people in formal arts education and representation has led some, even among us, to believe we are a people lacking in artistic or imaginative culture, and so limited in political requirements.

A lack of access and pessimistic stereotypes can shape tastes and limit expectations; that's true. It's difficult to become a fine wine or fine art aficionado when there are fewer viewing platforms available and less leisure time overall, and regardless, these things are no better than a dedication to lager and television. But, other than the significant impact of access and means, there is nothing inherent to being working class that prescribes any one set of tastes or behaviours and perhaps it is believing this to be the case that fuels the thinking behind cutting or withholding services and arts funding in working class areas in the first place, narrowing worlds to stereotypical visions.

Our stories are seldom told; working class fiction has seen some small bubblings of popularity, perhaps last fashionable in a limited way in the 90s, but for the most part, ranging from the glossy catalogues of publishers across the UK to what's covered on civilised radio review, working class stories are disproportionately absent.

I have read a lot of fiction straight from luxurious writing retreats; I have read almost none from housing estates such as the one I grew up on. These stories are missing, from shelves, and from the record. And further to this absolute travesty, for the sake of recording people in their multifaceted depths, broadening outlook, and for the integrity of literature itself – all the stories that might be missing, all the great works of literature that we might never read, or may never even hear about (because an editor cannot see its merit, or assumes there is no appetite), even fewer of these stories appear to be by women.

The Vida count tirelessly covers the gender breakdown of review publications; women are still not reviewed as often by literary publications, and other studies have shown stories focusing on women less likely to win prestigious awards. There are exceptions to the lack of female working class stories – glorious and affirming exceptions, such as the phenomenon of Elena Ferrante, or the stories of Pat Barker. But the working class voice, where it does exist, not limited to books but also in journalism and broadcasting, often takes on a male cast – and a white, straight one at that. Now and throughout history there are too few working class writers; and, as always, too few working class writers representing the cultural diversity of working class experience, where few of them manage to break through at all. Even in publishing, with a majority female workforce, structural inequality has seen gatekeeper positions, the highest earning heads of departments and editors, disproportionately male.

When I was a working class girl, born in the mid-80s, I learned to find joy in simple, inexpensive things, honing my observational powers, and I read every book I managed to get my hands on in flurries of utter love for words, art, and imagination. Thin as they were, I matched some working class schoolgirl stereotypes but rejected many more. I looked for stories reflecting my own experience or one like it, but found few; like women, working class, and other minority people throughout history looking on to a default perspective recorded on the shelves, one that was not our own.

I'm heartened by attempts to redress this by some activists and politicians, and the many unsung arts workers and individuals who recognise the importance to people and to the richness of art itself to broaden the range of stories being told, instigating funding drives, campaigns to save libraries, and publishing or curating more widely.

How many artists and writers have we never known, how many songs never sung, locked out by societal inequality? How many contributions by women have never been seen? How poorer are we all for that? In a strange and shifting global political climate, when clouds of austerity and xenophobia threaten to regress the tide of access to arts and literature, it is more important than ever before to keep rowing, hard as it may be, singing our own and varied songs, pushing against the stream.

GO HOME

Sim Bajwa

'And you know, I'm not afraid of being called a racist,' he says in a strong Brummie accent. 'It's not something I run from. It's people like the EDL, smashing up cars, vandalising shops, that give everyone a bad name.'

It's 2012, and I'm 20 years old. I'm tucked away in a corner table in Costa on campus, working my way through a pile of reading for an essay I left way too late. Hearing this, I freeze.

'I mean… as long as you're not violent, it's just an opinion, right? The thing is, when all these immigrants come over here, they set up these ghettos. Everyone's the same race, they won't learn English, freezing everyone else out. That's what my problem is. I just don't believe multiculturalism works. I think it actually divides society more. It's failed.'

Say something.

My face is hot and my heart is hammering. I'm angry, but I'm afraid to speak up, and equally afraid that if I do, I'll be dismissed. That they will look at each other and smirk.

Of course she thinks we're wrong. She's Asian.

I'm so taken aback by this conversation, by his poor attempt to intellectualise his racism, that I don't even know how to react.

'If I don't give a job to an Indian or an African, I don't think that makes me a bad person. It's this PC culture. It makes people feel like they have to accommodate everyone. I just think that we should put British culture first. They should understand that. I don't have a problem with anyone, but I do think we would get on better if people just stayed in their own countries. I don't think there's anything wrong with saying that.'

I look over at him. White guy on the next table. My age. Smile on his face, latte in front of him. His two friends – both also white men – sit across from him. One nods and chuckles every now and again, the other looks slightly uncomfortable.

Do they know I'm sitting here? Is he saying this on purpose?

It's clear he has no idea. He hasn't noticed me.

Say *something*.

'Oh, but don't get me wrong,' he says, with an easy laugh. He sips his coffee. 'I love Peking duck.'

Fast forward to late 2016, and I've just turned 24. It's been a weird, scary year. I've finished my postgraduate degree, and I'm figuring out what I should do next. I'm trying to keep positive about humanity in general, even though it feels like every new week is battering away at that optimism. I'm also more aware than I have ever been about who my parents are, and the parts of their lives I've only ever heard about.

I am first generation British–Indian, the oldest of three children. My parents left Punjab, India in the early 90s, and settled in Slough, England. An industrial town, about twenty miles west of London, it's one of the most ethnically diverse places in the UK. I spoke Punjabi before I spoke English. My neighbours were from a mix of backgrounds and I went to a very diverse school. We would exchange Christmas cards with our friends and family, and we would give our neighbours Indian food at Diwali. And yes, I suppose it would be exactly what White Guy In Costa carelessly referred to as a 'ghetto'. As evidence for the failure of multiculturalism.

My parents were my age when they immigrated. They'd just had an arranged marriage. To me, this isn't an unusual beginning, it's actually very common. The vast majority of my extended family in the UK and North America started their early twenties in exactly this way.

Slough is very different to where my parents grew up. My

dad is from Mustafabad, a rural village of almost 900 people. My mum is from Rayya, a larger town which is currently in transition from rural to urban. Most of their family is still there. In comparison, England must have been busy, loud, impatient, grey, and overwhelmingly foreign. The people look and act differently, speak a different language, and so many don't want you in their country. I imagine it would have been a comfort to live in a community where people spoke your language, made the food you were used to, practiced the same religion, and would help you to adjust to your new home.

I wonder how small your world must be, White Guy in Costa, how lacking in empathy and understanding, to see a community of people finding home in one another, and only see that they are not like you. To only focus on the fact that they're foreign, they don't speak English, they dress differently, they have different cultural norms, so they should not be here. To ignore the boldness and bravery that it must take to start a new life thousands of miles from everything familiar.

My parents both left school at around 16 years old, and don't have any formal qualifications. They taught themselves English. Before I was born, my mum used to work in a supermarket, stocking shelves, and my dad worked outside on a farm. The house that they lived in, the one that they eventually bought and I grew up in, was bare. They had no furniture, and the kitchen was just a portable gas cooker and a counter top. They would often go to my aunt's house for meals. My dad would cut the grass in the garden with a pair of kitchen scissors because they couldn't afford a lawn mower yet. My mum got a better job in a factory that packaged pens. They both passed their driving tests and my dad started driving a lorry, delivering building materials.

Over the years, they worked tirelessly, saved their money meticulously, and slowly but surely filled their home. They saved enough money to buy their own lorry, allowing my dad to become self-employed. Then, they saved enough to buy another one. And then another one. Now, they own their own business, one that they built from nothing. They have employees.

I don't remember any of the empty early years. I've seen some of this life in pictures, and I've heard stories, but none of it felt real to me when I was a teenager. In the childhood I remember, I don't lack anything. I don't recall feeling like anything was missing. My brothers and I got new school uniforms every year, we received birthday presents, we were gifted Christmas presents, we went on school trips, to the seaside in the summer, we were safe and loved. We were never hungry. My parents never let us feel like they couldn't provide anything we needed.

Maybe this is why I used to feel detached from the stories of their childhoods and their first few years in England. They talked about having little, but I had everything. How could I possibly understand what a big deal it was to my parents to buy my brother a bike? How could I understand the incredible freedom they gave me as an Indian girl, in a culture where it's harder to be a woman? That's not to say they didn't have traditional views on gender. They did, and still do. For a lot of years, I felt like I fought constantly to choose my own path. I'm still pushing against expectations that they have for me. But I never felt unsafe or scared to be myself, as untraditional as I am. I never felt like I'm sure many of my female cousins, and millions of girls I don't know, feel.

It's now, as a 24-year-old Indian woman in the 21st century, that I understand. If I had everything, it's because they worked to make it so. If I now have two university degrees, it's because they crossed continents and oceans so that I would have more opportunities than they did.

I can't know for sure what my life in India would have been like, but I probably would have been raised in my dad's village. It's unlikely I would have gone onto higher education. I might have been married off by now, and living with my in-laws. Maybe I'd even have children. I would have had to work harder for less, and there is no way I would have as much freedom as I have in the UK. It's not a reach to assume that I would have been told from birth that my role was ultimately to be a wife and a mother. Any children I had probably wouldn't have had access to the opportunities that I've taken for granted. I had the security to wear what I wanted, to identify as an atheist, to contradict family members older than me, to watch and read whatever I wished. It wouldn't have been so easy in an Indian village.

It's strange to know that everything that I am passionate about, and all the ambitions I have are only available to me because my parents are immigrants. It leaves me feeling grateful and humbled. To cross half the world, to live peacefully next to people fundamentally different from yourself, to make a place for yourself in a new society, while holding onto your culture, to give your children their best chance, is not a failure to me.

It's beautiful. It's a triumph.

2016 was tough, socially and politically, for a lot of people. I know it's naïve and idealistic, but I've always believed that good and fair wins eventually. While evil exists, most people try to do the right thing, and I believe that we are gradually heading in the right direction. But the last couple of years have hurt my faith and my heart.

Immigration has become a dirty word in mainstream media and politics. I went through the months leading up to the 2015 General Election with rising trepidation. *Surely people aren't going to vote Conservative,* I thought. *Not after the last five years. Surely people are going to dismiss Farage and UKIP. Remember Nick Griffin, made into a laughing stock in 2009? Farage isn't going to achieve anything.*

But every time I heard someone say how Farage 'seems like a normal bloke' and how he's 'right about some things', I felt afraid. Every time Ed Miliband and David Cameron mentioned a harder line on immigration, trying to sway potential UKIP voters, my fear grew.

Go Home

Forget about tax avoidance, forget about the richest continually screwing over the poorest, forget about cuts to welfare, it's immigrants who are the problem. People like my parents.

Brexit was pushed onto the British public with this rhetoric. *We don't have enough space. We don't have enough housing. We don't have enough jobs. They're stealing our benefits. They're bringing crime. They're destroying our culture. It's our country.*

Us. Our. Them.

It feels like a betrayal, first by politicians, and then by the general public.

I understand that not everyone who voted to leave the EU did it because of immigration. I do believe though, that racists and xenophobes have taken Brexit as a permission slip, as legitimisation of their beliefs. The wave of hate crimes show that they believe that the country is on their side.

To them, to the likes of Nigel Farage, it doesn't matter that my parents are British citizens, that they've lived in this country for longer than they lived in India. It doesn't matter how hard they've worked.

This was driven home to me in the summer of 2016 by reports of Byron Hamburgers' actions against their own employees. The company set up a fake training day for their kitchen staff, where it turned over employees to the Home Office in an immigration sting.[1] People who had worked for the company for years, some working 50 to 70 hours per week, were herded out of the building. They didn't get to say goodbye, they weren't allowed to go to their houses. They were ripped out of their lives. Everything they had worked for, everything they had built – gone. And of course, I think about my parents. I can imagine how powerless they would feel, how angry and scared and sad. The clear message here is that the lives of immigrants aren't as

---

1 '"It was a fake meeting": Byron Hamburgers staff on immigration raid', *The Guardian*, 28 July 2016, www.theguardian.com/uk-news/2016/jul/28/it-was-a-fake-meeting-byron-hamburgers-staff-on-immigration-raid.

important or valuable. Not to their employers, and certainly not to the government.

The rhetoric of immigrants being thieves, terrorists, rapists, as intrinsically Other, is being perpetuated by people in power who have no idea what it is to be an immigrant. Nowhere is this truer than in Donald Trump's victory in the US election. Again, like Brexit, not everyone who voted for Trump is a racist. However, his whole campaign was based on hatred, on setting up an Other to blame for the problems of the working class, on stirring up violence and anger. Us versus Them. To vote for him, to have treated him as a legitimate candidate in the first place, to act as if his inflammatory comments are debatable, is to be complicit in his exclusive version of America. Stories in the news of attacks on Muslims and immigrants in the US are horrific. I've tried to understand how people could vote for a monster but I can't. He never hid his bigotry. He said very clearly that he would ban Muslims and refugees from entering the United States. With the Executive Order he signed in January 2017, he did just that.[2] People's lives, security, and families snatched away, for no other crime than being an immigrant. The utter lack of shame and decency that it takes to do this is sickening. I'm scared and grieving for anyone in the US who isn't white, straight, cis, male, and able-bodied. The terror is bone deep.

In my mind, this attitude is distilled in something George Osborne said during Prime Minister's Questions in January 2016: 'We all enjoy a great British curry, but what we want are curry chefs trained here in Britain so we're providing jobs for people here in this country, and that's what our immigration controls provide.'[3] It was widely mocked online and compared

---

2 'Trump's Executive Order On Immigration, Annotated', *NPR*, 31 January 2017, www.npr.org/2017/01/31/512439121/trumps-executive-order-on-immigration-annotated.

3 'Who killed the great British curry house?', *The Guardian*, 12 January 2017, www.theguardian.com/lifeandstyle/2017/jan/12/who-killed-the-british-curry-house.

to Rowan Atkinson's skit in *Not the Nine O'Clock News* where his Tory MP character says, 'Now a lot of immigrants are Indians and Pakistanis for instance, and, I like curry, but now that we've got the recipe… is there really any need for them to stay?'.[4]

It's funny, but really, where's the lie? They want our things – our food, our labour, our money – but they don't want us.

It's infuriating and saddening. Underneath it all though, I'm weary. I'm tired of the dehumanisation of immigrants and the erasure of their experiences. I'm tired of knowing that when people mean 'immigrants' in the West, they don't mean white migrants from North America or Australia. I'm tired of feeling like I need to justify why my parents are here.

They learned English, they pay taxes, they've never been in trouble with the law, they've given me everything.

I shouldn't feel like I need to reel off this litany every time someone questions whether immigration is good or bad. How do I explain to someone who has no idea what it's like to live between two cultures? How can I make them see that it's rich and challenging and wonderful, all at the same time?

I'll never forget a conversation I had with a girl that I lived with during my undergraduate studies. The first time she met someone who wasn't white was when she moved away to university. She didn't know much about other cultures, and nor did she care to learn. Any experience outside of her white, middle class bubble was so far away from her life that I don't think she thought of it as real. She was another who questioned whether multiculturalism is a good thing. Never mind the fact that she'd had an Indian takeaway the night before. I jokingly answered that without multiculturalism, we wouldn't have *Bend*

---

4 'People are comparing George Osborne's comments on curry at PMQs to this Not the Nine O'Clock News sketch', *indy100*, www. indy100.com/article/people-are-comparing-george-osbornes-comments-on-curry-at-pmqs-to-this-not-the-nine-oclock-news-sketch--WyxjivHQc5l.

It Like Beckham, and wouldn't that be a shame?

She kept going though, and asked me if I thought multiculturalism actually worked, if I believed diversity was a positive part of British society. She talked about how uncomfortable she felt around people who spoke a language she didn't understand, and how she thought it would be best if people 'just stayed with their own kind'. When I pointed out that I'm one of those people, and questioned if she thought I didn't belong where I was, she told me I was different. I was different because I'd assimilated to British society. I didn't know how to make her understand that yes, I had, but also, no, I haven't. I walk between two cultures that are opposites. I switch between English and Punjabi with ease. I pick and choose aspects from each side of my life, depending on what I identify with. This is true for my parents as well who grew up with one culture, and then had to learn to live in another. They found a balanced middle ground. And this experience is in no way unique to my family. Over ten percent of the UK are immigrants and more than half of this group aren't white.[5] These people, their children, their grandchildren, are absolutely, undeniably British.

My former housemate's mindset is one that I've encountered time and again, personally and in the media. Difference is bad. Difference is dangerous. I'm lucky that I've had little malicious racism directed at me. The most I've experienced are micro-aggressions of the 'Where are you really from?' and 'You're getting an arranged marriage, right?' and 'You're a Muslim, yeah?' and 'I wouldn't say that you're Indian, I would say you're English' variety. Sometimes it's in making me feel as if I'm so very different, and sometimes it's in erasing my identity in an effort to find a cultural box to fit me in. Day to day, I don't

5 '2011 Census analysis: Ethnicity and religion of the non-UK born population in England and Wales', *Office for National Statistics,* 18 June 2015. www.ons.gov.uk/peoplepopulationandcommunity/culturalidentity/ethnicity/articles/2011censusanalysisisethnicityandreligionofthenonukbornpopulationinenglandandwales/2015-06-18.

feel like I don't belong, or that my family isn't British. Instead, it's in the moment where a politician stokes anti-immigration sentiments and large groups of people respond positively. The moment where my ethnicity and my parents' background is treated as a taboo subject, the moment a man yelled 'GO HOME, YOU FUCKING PAKI' in my face as I crossed the road in Birmingham. The moment that I realised my Prime Minister will smile and walk hand in hand with Trump before condemning his actions as racist, fascist, and inhumane.[6]

It's in the moments I realise that for a lot of people, yes, my family is British, but... We belong here, but... It's an uncomfortable in-between where I never quite feel on level ground. I'm expected to feel grateful towards a country that has given me a better life than I would have had otherwise, but the idea of feeling grateful towards Britain makes me feel as though we're in a host country, rather than our own. We have to give back more than those who aren't a product of immigration. We have to earn our place here. We have to never give anyone a chance to say that we shouldn't be here.

Sometimes, it feels like rebellion to claim our space without apology. To me, Britain is multicultural, and better for it. I was silent in 2012 because trying to change White Guy's mind felt futile, but you can bet I won't be quiet now. I might be lucky to be born in Britain, but Britain is lucky to have my parents. I wouldn't trade being the daughter of immigrants for the world. I couldn't. It makes me feel indescribably proud to look around their home and our lives, and think about how they built it all themselves. It makes me feel like, if they can do all this, I can do anything.

---

6   'Lie Back and Think of England', *Pacific Standard*, 1 February 2017. www.psmag.com/what-theresa-may-has-lost-by-pandering-to-trump-769dbc872cd7#.j1yrov14u.

LOVE IN A TIME OF MELANCHOLIA

Becca Inglis

Courtney Love
trash
n.

Worthless or discarded material or objects; refuse or rubbish.

Something broken off or removed to be discarded, especially plant trimmings.

The refuse of sugar cane after extraction of the juice.

A place or receptacle where rubbish is discarded: threw the wrapper in the trash.

Empty words or ideas.

Worthless or offensive literary or artistic material.

Disparaging, often abusive speech about a person or group.

A person or group of people regarded as worthless or contemptible.

by bebo January 07, 2005, Urban Dictionary[1]

1. She's the angel on top of the tree

Courtney Love lives inside a dark mirror. For the past decade, her life has played itself out on flat surfaces, first on the glossy pages of magazines before moving behind the glass pane on

---

1 'Courtney Love', *Urban Dictionary*, www.urbandictionary.com/define.php?term=Courtney+Love&defid=984711.

computer screens. She is not a rounded character but has instead been reduced to flat archetypes that can be found in their most natural habitat, the depths of the YouTube comment section. Nobody is sure which is the real Courtney, and which is the reflection. One is a grunge princess, a Cinderella who married grunge's Prince Charming Kurt Cobain, but tried to win over the people with her own intellect and spark. The other is a mad witch, a murderous queen jealous of those with more power and fame. Each has its own loyal band of followers, who are locked in a fierce war of words defending their version of the rock star.

I was already looking for Courtney when she hurtled into my world. Unlike her original fans, I did not stumble on her band's LP, *Live Through This*, while rifling through record shops or reading about her scandalous relationships on the cover of *Spin*.[2] I am too young to remember Courtney's heyday in the headlines or the waves that she made in modern feminism. Yet, much like those first admirers in the nineties, I was starved of female icons.

I did not like being in my own skin. It was painfully shy, bookish, and plain. It did not stand up next to the pretty girls at school, who knew what music to listen to and how to pass tests without seeming too clever. They modelled themselves on Britney Spears or Cameron Diaz or Gwyneth Paltrow, but I felt like a far cry from those sophisticated, popular, blonde, and bronzed A-listers. I was looking for a way to be in the world, women who would show me how to break out of my misfit status. Rock, which traditionally belongs to the alienated, spoke to me on some levels, but at this point I did not know about riot grrrl, or Kathleen Hanna, or The Runaways. There was a palpable woman-shaped hole in the music and I, new to the genre, was desperately trying to fill it.

And there she was, on my television screen, an accidentally-

---

2   Cooper, Dennis. 'Love Conquers All.' *Spin*, May 1994.

on-purpose arrival. I was not searching at that precise moment, but I recognised what I had been looking for straight away. In the music video for 'Celebrity Skin', which Hole first released in March 1998, Courtney preens in a red ball gown under a shower of gold glitter dust, her platinum curls a dishevelled frame around her face. She is almost the picture of California princess, except for her raw voice lamenting 'My name is never was'. She is blonde in a different way. She is not sun-kissed but messy, bleached until scorched, unhappy. When she sings about Hollywood, it is about being an outsider, about teeth rotting on sugar.

It was one of those moments that makes you sit bolt upright, blows you back into your seat from the aftershock. When the video finished, in the quiet after the storm, I knew I had found my answer. There was a woman who I could follow. That was who I could be.

2. Burn the witch

Loving Courtney is not easy. Many of her actions over the years have been at least questionable, and do not add up to the ideal role model held up by her fans. She is a notorious addict, has lost custody of her daughter multiple times, was the first person to be sued for Twitter libel. Some have fallen out of love with Courtney altogether, with one blogger formally bidding farewell to her in the article 'How the Love Was Lost'. After years of watching her icon drift through legal courts and rehabilitation centres, Hannah Levin deemed Courtney too far strayed from the path to defend anymore.[3]

A distinct anxiety surrounds celebrity role models. We paint them as gods amongst us, a blueprint for how we behave, and when they show human error they are hurriedly cast out.

---

3   Levin, Hannah. 'How the Love Was Lost: A Career Eulogy from a Former Fan.' *The Stranger*, 20 November 2003.

In 2015, the website Vouchercloud published results from a survey on parents' favourite celebrity icons. At the top of the list was Kate Middleton, a fine example of beauty and grace.[4] At the opposite end of the spectrum was Miley Cyrus, who had abruptly transformed herself from clean teen pop star to gyrating party animal at the VMAs the year before. Parents were incensed by Miley dressing up as a teddy bear and simulating masturbation, while vocal feminists like Sinead O'Connor and Annie Lennox were concerned that by twerking on Robin Thicke she was conceding to sexism in the music industry.[5]

Sometimes the role model you need is not an example to aspire to, but someone who reflects back the parts of yourself that society deems unfit. When I first discovered Hole, I was delighted to find a photo of Courtney when she was the same age as me, similarly round-faced, sturdy, and awkward looking. Fast forward to her thirties, and Courtney becomes a much more complicated role model. Kati Nolfi describes the unique experience of being a Hole fan in her review of Anwen Crawford's book *Hole's Live Through This*.[6] Straying into the noxious comments section on YouTube and news sites, you simultaneously cringe at your idol and become fiercely defensive. Courtney's fans are 'ambivalent' to their 'problematic fave'.[7]

Having a 'problematic fave', I think, is what helped me navigate the black moods that fogged over so much of my young life. Even as a child, I displayed neurotic traits that preclude

---

4   Crain, Esther. 'Miley Cyrus Tops the List of Worst Celebrity Role Models for Kids.' *Yahoo! News*, 26 August 2015.
5   Williams, Rhiannon. 'Annie Lennox 'disturbed and dismayed' by overtly sexualised pop performances.' *The Telegraph*, 6 October 2013.
6   Crawford, Anwen. *Hole's Live Through This*. London: Bloomsbury Academic, 2014. 33 1/3.
7   Nolfi, Kati. '*Hole's Live Through This* by Anwen Crawford.' *Bookslut*, April 2015.

depression – an intensely low self-esteem, a heightened anxiety about abandonment, sensitivity to criticism – and the older I grew, the further I teetered over the shadowy pit's edge. Steeped as her life has been in mental illness, either her husband's or speculation over her own, Courtney was a sort of dark beacon when at last I fell.

Courtney stands accused of Kurt Cobain's murder. It is rock's favourite debate: is she guilty or innocent? So much so that when you (often Othered, often a woman) say that you like her music, you automatically brace for a reaction. 'She killed Kurt, and he wrote her songs.'

Before Kurt's death in 1994, his wife was painted as an opportunistic groupie hungry for his fame and jealous of his talent. Pale-skinned and red mouthed, she was a vampire draining him of his intellectual and financial wealth. After he died, Courtney inherited an estimated $130 and $115 million respectively of Kurt's writing and publishing rights,[8] and people also noted how quickly she went back to work. *Live Through This* was released just one week after Kurt's body was found, which proved to many a lack of remorse, maybe even a motive. It looked like Courtney felt nothing for Kurt at all, was capitalising on the news of his death to promote her album.[9] She was the evil queen who outlived her husband, not beautiful, but ugly, inside and out.

Unfeeling, impulsive, ambitious. It is easy to pathologise the accusations that are thrown at Courtney. Her own estranged father, Hank Harrison, asserted his belief that his daughter was a murderer to NBC News: 'She's a psychopath, she has a sociopathic personality like I do.' Psychopaths are famously

---

8 Weisman, Aly. 'Courtney Love Already "Lost About $27 Million" Of Her "Nirvana Money"', *Business Insider*, 11 August 2014. http://www. businessinsider.com/courtney-love-lost-27-million-of-nirvana-money-2014-8?IR=T.

9 'Courtney Love, murderous psychopath.' *Lucky Otters Haven*, 31 May 2015.

impulsive, parasitic, egomaniacal, cut-throat, and calculating. They are the bogeymen of our popular imagination, our most notorious killers and terrifying monsters. In everyday life they are attracted to positions of power, where they manipulate for their own gain.[10] Harrison commented of his son-in-law, 'I know who benefited from his death: my daughter, for one.'[11]

It should be said that Courtney has never publicly disclosed a mental illness diagnosis, although critics often reference the therapist who sued her in 2014 for unpaid bills.[12] Courtney's perceived mental health issues are bound up with her nastiness, an accusation bandied about alongside misogynistic snipes. It is difficult not to point out that Kurt shared many of Courtney's faults (addiction, questionable parenting, self-destruction) but comparatively gets off scot-free. For a woman who has also experienced depression, this coalescence of mental health stigma and sexism makes it easy to empathise with Courtney. For me, growing up, she has always felt like a distant ally. Looking at her, in all her forms behind the looking glass, I felt less alone in the mist.

3. Someday you will ache like I ache

One of the most often quoted psychologists on 'celebrity worship' is Dr John Maltby, who has built on research done by Lynn E. McCutcheon that links three personality types with the phenomenon: the entertainment-social dimension – the hobbyist who shares a casual interest with their friends; the borderline-pathological dimension – associated with wild fantasies and compulsive, sometimes self-destructive, acts of

---

10   Robinson, Kara Mayer. 'Sociopath vs. Psychopath: What's the Difference?', *WebMD*, n.d.

11   Lauer, Matt. 'More questions in Kurt Cobain death?', NBC News, 4 May 2004.

12   Newman, Jason. 'Courtney Love Sued by Psychiatrist for 'Breach of Contract", *Rolling Stone*, 25 February 2014.

love; and the intense-personal dimension – the one who finds things in common, and might begin to mimic the star.[13] Maltby et al. surveyed 372 men and women around the UK about the extent of their celebrity worship, coping style, and general life satisfaction. They found a significant correlation between depression and anxiety and the intense-personal dimension.[14] The intense-personal dimension is characterised by a stable and global attributional style, meaning that incidents are viewed as beyond the person's control and linked to pervasive factors.[15] It is easy to draw the line to depression. One of its most famous sufferers, Vincent Van Gogh, wrote to his brother of his torment and helplessness: 'One feels as if one were lying bound hand and foot at the bottom of a deep dark well, utterly helpless'.[16]

Depression is a black hole out of which you are too tired to climb. Overgeneralising and catastrophising are typical of the depressed, where you see one isolated incident as linked to several bad events and blow the whole thing out of proportion.[17] The negative self-talk forms a clamour in your head so loud, and so confusing, that you cannot begin to fathom how to get out. A deep resignation sets in where you cannot find joy, or even real sadness, and become apathetic to the prospect of recovery. Preoccupied with the damning narrative in your

13   McCutcheon, Maltby, J. P. Houran, & Diane D. Ashe. *Celebrity worshippers: Inside the minds of stargazers*. Frederick, MD: Publish America, 2004.

14   Maltby, Liza Day, McCutcheon, Raphael Gillett, James Houran, and Ashe. 'Personality and coping: A context for examining celebrity worship and mental health.' *British Journal of Psychology*. 2004, 95: pp. 411–428.

15   North, Adrian C., Lorraine Sheridan, Maltby and Gillett. 'Attributional Style, Self-Esteem, and Celebrity Worship.' *Media Psychology*, 2007 (9.2): pp. 291–308.

16   Popova, Maria. 'Van Gogh and Mental Illness.' *Brain Pickings*, 5 June 2014.

17   Gilbert, Paul. 'Depression: A Self-help Guide.' Moodjuice, 2009.

head, inferior to your peers, disengaged from your loved ones – depression is the loneliest feeling in the world. I have often felt like I am watching the world through a dirty window, or a black embryonic wall impossible to pierce through.

Courtney has embodied several kinds of loneliness. She was briefly one half of a pair, but then suddenly left alone to navigate single parenthood, widowhood, and an addiction to heroin. Her erratic behaviour and substance abuse caused her only daughter Frances Bean Cobain to legally emancipate herself from her mother in 2009.[18] Wars over ownership of the Nirvana estate led to Courtney's long and bitter feud with drummer Dave Grohl, also her long-time friend. She has been questioned in interviews over rumours about her involvement in Kurt's death, been in several toxic relationships since, and faced constant scrutiny over her vulgarity.

In one such interview with the television show *Rage*, Courtney confirmed that she had written 'Doll Parts' about Kurt. When they first started dating, Courtney feared that Kurt did actually not like her, and so wrote a song about unrequited love and rejection.[19] This sense of abandonment took on a more pronounced meaning after Kurt's death. Hole's bassist Patty Schemel has said of the *Live Through This* tour, 'certain things would remind her, a lot of the time on-stage, and it would just come out. Certain lyrics had a lot more meaning.'[20]

When I listened to 'Doll Parts' at the age of seventeen, I was not yet officially diagnosed with depression. The illness was more a hint on my periphery, having googled it once two years before to see if it might explain my chronic sadness. Since starting college, my social calendar had been driven by the prospect of a

---

18   Rosenberg, Alyssa. 'Courtney Love Is In Trouble Again. Why Do I Still Care?', *Slate*, 4 October 2012.

19   Creswell, Toby. *1001 Songs*. Melbourne: Hardie Grant Publishing, October 2009.

20   Gottlieb, Sean. *Courtney Love: Behind the Music*. VH1, 2010.

fresh start, the chance to get invited to parties, to be well-liked and accepted. Whereas before I had been excruciatingly tongue-tied, now I talked to everyone, allowing my mouth to run on in a frantic attempt to negate any awkward silences.

This should have been a happier time, and in some ways it was. Taking inspiration from Courtney, I started colouring my eyes black and bleaching my dishwater blonde hair. I wore tulle skirts with big boots, and felt powerful as I stomped around college in statement evening gowns. For once I felt pretty, like I had things to say that wouldn't make people scoff. I was starting to gain courage, even to like parts of myself.

But with new friends comes greater visibility. There is more potential for failure when you put yourself out there, and I was braced for it every time I opened my mouth. I was convinced that I had hit on some secret formula for making people like me, and that to deviate from it would mean plunging back into invisibility. I styled my hair, made witty quips, and sought out parties at the weekends not for fun, but out of an intense desperation not to be alone. That permanent state of defence is not sustainable. All fortresses under siege risk draining their resources. Loneliness seeps into everything, and every solitary moment feels like evidence that you are unlovable. Whenever I found myself alone, my fortification became brittle and I succumbed to negative self-talk. Hate is a word that used to crop up a lot. I despised my sensitivity and pessimism, felt that I was pathetic because everyone else was so much better at living.

Listening to Courtney was cathartic. My own fears of social isolation and the scornful disengagement from myself were being played out on a stage. When Courtney sings 'I am doll parts', she turns herself into a living doll that is malleable putty in Kurt's hands. He can love her one minute and then toss her out when he grows tired of her, and Courtney is helplessly resigned to her friendless fate. There is a raw balance between apathy and pain in the couplet 'It stands for knife/For the rest of my life'. The knife cuts through the rest of the song's weary lyrics, and Courtney gives up hope of it ever going away. The impassive doll matched my own listlessness, the dark well that I found myself in.

Reaching across the audiosphere, Courtney's voice made me feel less like an oddity and more like I was part of a club. It was comforting to know that I shared these thoughts with someone else. The psychiatrist Irvin Yalom lists this sense of universality as one of eleven curative factors in group therapy.[21] By hearing other people relate their experiences to you, you begin to realise that you are not alone in your impulses and feelings. Your experiences are validated. They are part and parcel of everyday human experiences. You are not mad or hysterical or awful but regular, part of a group that quietly muddles through life together. Having discovered that you are not uniquely bad, you can start to feel better about yourself.

In Crawford's book *Hole's Live Through This*, she interviews Hole fans about the impact that the album had on their teenage lives.[22] One word that turns up a lot is 'permission'. Courtney, harshly naked in her lyrics and resolutely unapologetic about her divisive behaviour, gives her fans permission to be themselves, to be a woman, be slutty, be fat, ugly, pretty, gay, loud, angry, feminine, intellectual, outrageous. Reading that word, I too feel a jolt of recognition. It took me years to get my depression diagnosed. Ex-boyfriends have called me crazy, my peers have called me a freak, a stupid emo, an attention-seeker. I have believed that I am mad, considered running away or never leaving the house again. Courtney gave me permission to feel sad in a world where mental illness is viewed as mere navel gazing, selfishness, drama, and weakness. This sort of stigma can

21   Yalom, Irvin. *The Theory and Practice of Group Psychotherapy*. 5th ed. New York: *Basic Books*, 2005.
22   Crawford, Anwen. *Hole's Live Through This*. London: Bloomsbury Academic, 2014. 33 1/3.

be devastating for a person trying to get well. Already sensitive to criticism and self-loathing, stereotypes about mental illness make it difficult to confide in anyone, even to seek treatment.[23] It is impossible to know who is a friend and who would cast you out as a worthless freak.

Courtney approaches mental illness the same way that she does being a woman: angry defiance. 'Doll Parts' is actually split into two parts. In the first, she is soft and helpless, a victim to the rejection she feels from Kurt and his obsessive fans. In the second half, she practically shouts 'I am doll parts'. She is affirmative, taking pride in her fragile edges. The refrain 'Someday you will ache like I ache' before was sad and quiet. Now she screams it, like a hex launched at her critics.

One of my favourite quotes from Courtney turns the alienated and depressed self on its head. 'Don't be bitter and mean cos you don't fit in,' she says, 'it's a GIFT. Look at you. you've got your individuality, you don't have the herd instinct, you can read Nietzsche and understand it. Only dumb people are happy.'[24]

4. Live through this with me

Unfortunately, even after recovery, over half of people who have experienced a major depressive episode will relapse. That likelihood increases with every episode, and most will suffer between five and nine in their lifetime.[25] The first time, when you have no prior experience of the feeling, depression sinks into your life without detection. The second time, depression is accompanied by a sense of dread as its cold fingers tendril

---

23   'Stigma and discrimination', *Mental Health Foundation*, www.mentalhealth.org.uk/a-to-z/s/stigma-and-discrimination.

24   Wright, Lisa. 'Courtney Love: 30 of Her Most Candid Quotes', *NME,* 18 March 2015.

25   Burcusa, Stephanie L. and William G. Iacono. 'Risk for Recurrence in Depression.' *Clinical Psychology Review,* 2007 27(8), pp. 959-985.

around the corners of your brain. You know this feeling. It is a familiar ghost that you thought you had managed to exorcise. When you remember what the wraith put you through last time, how it impacted your family or friends, you chastise yourself for allowing yourself to slip. You know that you are vulnerable, and you are meant to know what triggers it. You should have kept a tighter grip on things, been more vigilant. Clearly, thoughts like this will not help you leave the well, and are more likely to push you further under the water.

I have relapsed twice since I first conquered my black dog, and both times I have turned to Courtney. She is the soundtrack to my melancholia because she gives me the strength to pull myself out. Courtney's life is not one big mess, but a series of slip-ups in succession. Up and down she goes, kicking her heroin habit but then meeting Kurt, and spiralling into addiction again and again.[26]

For all her lying, cheating, and bad mothering, Courtney has taught me a valuable lesson: nobody is perfect. Not even the celebrities who you model yourself on as a teen, and keep admiring in your adulthood. You may not forgive Courtney, but you can accept her, and somehow that peace comes back to you. Relapse is normal, not proof that you are not fit for this world.

Over the past two years, Courtney has shown signs of a fresh recovery. She states that she has been clean since 2007 and is now a committed Buddhist – she credits her daily chanting as a lifeline that has helped her overcome drug cravings. In 2010, she released *Nobody's Daughter*, a redemptive album that sought to undo the mess that had been *America's Sweetheart* six years before (nicknamed 'le disaster' by Courtney, due to her addiction to crack whilst recording).[27] She starred in an

---

26 *Kurt Cobain: Montage of Heck*. Directed by Brett Morgan. Universal Pictures, April 2015.

27 *The Return of Courtney Love*. Directed by Will Yapp. More4, September 2006.

opera in 2015, which was widely heralded as a success, and quit smoking briefly so that she could commit to rehearsing.[28] A year later, she was reconciled with Dave Grohl[29] and with her estranged daughter, and she would go on to give one of her most candid interviews in *Kurt Cobain: Montage of Heck*, which Frances produced.

Yalom argues that hearing stories from others in group therapy can instil a sense of hope. By witnessing people who are further along the road to recovery than you, you can take comfort and even become optimistic about your own health. Nowadays, watching Courtney, you cannot help but feel that if she can do it, if she can recover from her husband's death, the murder accusations, the loss of her child, and drug addiction, then you can overcome your own demons, however big or small.

What defines Courtney is not her nastiness, or her relentless appetite for self-destruction. It is her resolve to keep living, even when she is walking through hell. In the introduction to *Dirty Blonde: The Diaries of Courtney Love*, her late friend Carrie Fisher described her many, if at times misguided, attempts to heal herself: 'After all is said and done – whenever that is – she is a survivor'.[30] Over and over again, Courtney springs back from the well. Whenever it looks like she has reached her limit, is in danger of destroying herself or fading into obscurity, somehow, she keeps going. In Courtney's version of mental illness there is an end in sight, and it does not involve a gun.

28 'Courtney Love & Todd Almond: The San Francisco Sessions.' *Groundbreakers with Kevin Sessums*. San Francisco Curran, 17 March 2016.

29 'Courtney Love/Chris Elliott/Rhiannon Giddens.' *Late Show with David Letterman*, written by R.J. Fried, Matt Kirsch, Paul Masella, and Zach Smilovitz. CBS, 10 February 2015.

30 Love, Courtney. *Dirty Blonde: Diaries of Courtney Love*. London: Faber and Faber, 2006.

Conclusion: Rose white, rose red

I have looked to a woman with flaws and many enemies. In spite of her wild image, Courtney is vulnerable. She struggles to cope, makes mistakes, has not always taken good care of herself. This is what makes her more real to me than other more 'suitable' role models. As Courtney and I have gone through the years, she has reassured me that illness is quite ordinary.

Of Vouchercloud's list of bad celebrity role models, Nicki Minaj has been called 'not too kind' by Miley Cyrus and 'savage' by Salon, Kristen Stewart has a 'bad attitude' and does not smile enough, and Miley herself, as we have seen, is too sexually explicit, too much in favour of a dangerous party lifestyle.[31][32] Yet Nicki was called those terms because she was venting her frustration at the racial bias in her industry (and then standing up for herself when Miley criticised her for the way she expressed her anger). Kristen has opened up about her struggles with anxiety, and also become more comfortable with the press since she revealed her relationships with other women. Miley openly identifies as gender neutral and pansexual, and has campaigned to raise awareness about homelessness in the young LGBTQ community. Melissa McLaren was particularly zealous when defending Miley in the Huffington Post: 'As the parent of a transgender 9-year-old girl, I was excited to share that Miley is very aware of gender issues and embraces a life free from the boxes we traditionally put people into … I'm thrilled that my daughter can call you a role model. Yep, I just said that. And meant it.'[33]

---

31   Mullin, Benjamin. 'Salon apologizes for calling Nicki Minaj's speech 'savage'.' *Poynter*, 31 August 2015.
32   Kim, Kristen Yoonsoo. 'The Moment Kristen Stewart Stopped Being Hollywood's Most Hated Actress.' *Complex*, 1 June 2016.
33   McLaren, Melissa. 'Why This Mom Is Calling Miley Cyrus a Hero.' *Huffington Post*, 11 May 2016.

Each of these women has faced an obstacle and fought hard to overcome it, be it opposition to their personality, or their identity, or the way that they oppose their oppression. Courtney, as noted by Touré in an interview for *Fuse*, is her own greatest barrier, which she is now also showing signs of surpassing.[34] That determination in the face of adversity, wherever it may come from, is surely something to be emulated and admired, not damned.

In one of Crawford's interviews, a fan of Hole named Nicole Solomon said, 'She's telling you not to be ashamed of yourself and to express yourself, including the parts of yourself that society may deem ugly and inappropriate.' When you feel ugly, inside or out, you might become ill, and if you become ill then some might see you as ugly. Courtney breaks that cycle, and guides you down the path to the end.

Courtney is a complicated role model to say the least. Loving her means accepting all her forms behind the glass, the princess and the hag and the somewhere in-between. It is that multi-faceted edge, that feeling of loose and trailing strings, that has made Courtney a star in the night for so many of us. We are imperfect selves with messy lives, or at least considered so by a status quo. If Maltby is right, and there is a strong link between identifying with famous people and depression, then it is messy celebrities that we need to help us navigate every hurdle.

---

34 'On the Record: Courtney Love.' *Fuse*, 11 March 2012.

CHOICES

Rowan C. Clarke

You can distil a life into a series of choices. You can't choose where and when you're born, of course, but you make choices and deal with the consequences of other people's choices in all the years after that.

You can choose to listen to the people around you.

Or you can choose not to.

You can choose to let people make decisions for you.

Or you can choose not to.

You can choose to take the path others want you to take.

Or you can choose not to.

I ended up choosing *not* to do many things that were expected of me and instead chose a path where I could fully be myself. Every single one of us is unique and we express our identities in our very own way, but we still need to fit into the society we live in. Growing up queer and independent in a small Mediterranean village wasn't easy. I think it says a lot more about the fragility of society as a whole – this pathological need to fit people neatly into two gender categories with all their rules and identifiers – than it says about those of us who choose to rebel against these rules. Girls like pink and girly things and need to please boys. Boys like blue and boyish things but need not please girls.

I was my parents' second child. I don't think my mother really wanted children, but having children was what you were meant to do when you got married, so that's what she did. She told me repeatedly throughout my childhood that having children had ruined her life. I heard it so many times growing up that I couldn't help but believe it. She couldn't stand it when my sister and I strayed from the narrative she had built in her head of what her family should be. I was doing most of the straying by being 'different', so I felt keenly that I had personally ruined my mother's life.

I always thought I had a relatively happy childhood in a relatively normal family. If anything, it felt more like there was a problem with *me*. It was always so hard to fit in and to please my mother. It felt like things I said or did always missed the mark. It is only when I left, travelled, met people, that I realised something wasn't quite right.

Growing up in my family was like living every day in ill-fitting clothes. I spent my time feeling uncomfortable and struggling to breathe. The mould I was expected to fit into impaired my very existence. Yet everyone around me was wearing similar clothes and it didn't seem to bother *them*. Why couldn't I just be like everyone else?

As a child I always loved reading. In stories, good people win. They *always* win. In stories there's usually only a handful of bad people trying to corrupt the good ones. Most people are good, normal people. If you don't fit in with the majority, then you're not one of the good people.

That's how it works. Or so I thought.

I grew up thinking I was a science experiment gone wrong, the evil child, the stranger moving amongst the good folks around me. I grew up scared of myself. I hated myself. My mother has always been very opinionated and everybody's actions were judged through her very particular morality lens. It was hard work to please my mother. She would get so enraged when I didn't act the way she wanted me to. She said I played the victim and was lazy when I didn't do what she said. Why couldn't I just be normal and make her proud?

She always had an 'us vs. them' vision of the world, in which she and our family were virtuous and everyone else was not. No one went unjudged, from family and friends to random people she didn't even know. Sometimes I was cast as one of *them*. She would be even more ruthless if I disappointed her in front of other people. How dare I show her up like that?

Food became a real issue for my mother. It wasn't about starving herself or vomiting. It was subtler than that. Every conversation she had seemed to revolve around food: how little she could eat, how full she felt, how fat some people are. At mealtimes, she always had to be the one to eat the least – it was the only way for her to win. This obsession extended to her daughters of course, my sister ready to follow, me a little less. They were both constantly dieting, judging me for not bothering. My mother's attitude to food had such an influence on me that for years I thought I was the one with an eating disorder.

I chose to acknowledge my difference

The more I tried, the less I managed to please. I felt the goalposts move each time I did something. My mother wanted me to lose weight. My mother wanted me to be girly. My mother wanted me to fit in. I tried to.

At the back of my head, there was something whispering to me that there had to be another way. But I didn't want to listen. I wanted to be *normal* and I felt monstrously abnormal. It's hard – practically impossible, really – to put a name on a feeling or a state of being when you're not given the tools to recognise it. See, I wasn't born an independent queer feminist – no one is – I was born in a society that forged me into one. I didn't realise until years later that what I felt, being treated differently to the boys around me, was inequality, pure and simple. Girls should work hard, be humble and shut their mouths. Girls should be girly but not too sexy. There are so many rules that come with being a girl that you forget sometimes that these rules are ficti-tious patriarchal bullshit. You're so intent on being the good girl everyone wants you to be that you forget to be yourself.

I had never cared much about my appearance but I was made to through years of intense scrutiny and criticism. Why couldn't I just be pretty? Didn't I want to be desirable to boys? My sister played the game, so why couldn't I? My sister *wanted* to be attractive and worked hard at it and was praised by my mother. My mother enlisted her to tell me to start making an effort with my appearance. My lack of interest always seemed so problematic to them. I remember their complete incredulity each summer when I chose to read my book inside instead of tanning in the sun like my sister. I was given sexy clothes as gifts, reminded that make-up existed, told to lose weight, quizzed about boyfriends. Why couldn't I be the girl they so desperately wanted me to be?

My mother often searched my room when I wasn't there, just in case my lack of interest in all things girly would reveal I was hiding *The Gay Agenda* and *I Heart Girls* paraphernalia under my bed. I was treated with such a degree of suspicion that I came to think something *must* be wrong with me.

My mother wanted to have the best family, yet she wasn't interested in the family she had. Nothing in her life was allowed to differ from the 'norm', whatever that is. Any hiccup or incident would be hushed up. She always had to be seen as the best mother and she would not allow her daughters to shame her. My mother's pride was its own form of nutrition and as her weight came down, her pride expanded.

I chose to hide who I was

As I came to realise that something in me was different, I knew I would just have to carry on disappointing my family. Around adolescence, through watching films and reading, I had a pretty good idea of what I wasn't. I also realised that no one would understand or accept me – I heard enough criticisms from my family on the subject to know they wouldn't be allies. It was exhausting to put on a mask every day but it became paramount for me to hide what I felt. I knew my life depended on it.

Nothing had changed on the outside and I still tried hard to fit in. But on the inside, it felt like a world of difference. I began to choose not to hate myself. It didn't happen overnight; there was no eureka moment. I just allowed myself to see me for who I was and I chose not to hate myself for it.

There were now two sides to me – the person they thought I was, and the real me. I thought of my feelings as being taboo, perverse and the result of a chemical imbalance – this is what the environment I grew up in taught me. The homophobia surrounding me was utterly toxic. I can still remember the creeping sense of unease I felt when I heard schoolmates saying that gay people should be rounded up and exterminated – repeating their parents' words, no doubt. It made me feel so alien to be something that was so horrifying for others. Often my family would discuss homosexuality with disgust, proclaiming they would never leave children anywhere near gay people.

There really is no way to grow up a healthy and delightfully queer child when you hear this type of language every day. I can remember listening to these conversations and feeling shame and fear at being discovered. It is so confusing to be attracted to girls while only knowing a heteronormative society and thinking those feelings were impossible.

Now I am old enough to know that the hate was never *really* about sexuality. It is more about society's 'natural order'. If some people don't fit in the 'natural order', they might trigger other people to question that order.

And no one wants that.

When I started to realise my feelings weren't going anywhere, I knew I had to leave. I knew deep down that if anyone knew who I was, I would be killed or be pushed to suicide. After all, I only knew of one other gay person in my neighbourhood and he was six feet under. I gradually pieced together my uncle's story by listening behind closed doors. He was gay, contracted AIDS in the 80s and killed himself. My family's shame was so great that they buried him in the night.

I chose to live

When I was left alone at home, I would often pick the biggest knife, thinking about what a relief it would be not to have to try so hard every day. I did little cuts, never breaking the skin, just to practise how it would feel. In public, I put on a smile. I shut down my feelings and worked hard to get away. Phase One of my quiet revolution.

I contemplated suicide many times. As any LGBTQ young person living in a narrow-minded community can tell you, a wholesome mind cannot be sustained through being forced into being someone you're not, all while fearing for your life.

I had the classic fantasy that one day someone would tell me that there had been a mix-up at the hospital and this wasn't my real family. But it wasn't a princess or a wizard that I wanted to be. What I craved was smaller, simpler: a family who loved me unconditionally. I always had the hope that despite everything, there was a future for me out there. (Spoiler alert: there was.)

One of the books that helped me was *The Crucible* by Arthur Miller. It resonated so much with me at the time and is one of the books I still cherish. I identified with John Proctor – funnily enough, not for the sexy times with the serving girls – but for his righteousness against all odds, despite everyone telling him he was wrong. Reading *The Crucible*, I realised that sometimes the good guys are the small minority and everyone else is being swept along on a tide of misguided morality.

Rowan C. Clarke

I chose exile

When I was around fifteen years old, I realised that I could not truly be myself until I was settled and financially independent. Yes, it was years away and yes, it would mean years of pain and the heartache of hiding who I was, always being on guard to field off all the questions and suspicions. But there was something in me that drove me to want a life for myself and to make a success of it. I secured a place at one of the best universities in the country – the first person in my family to enter higher education. This didn't go down well with my mother. Imagine, sending her shameful daughter away where she couldn't be controlled – what would she do? (As it turns out, not drugs and tantric sex trysts but more reading and studying. Queer youth is so wild, I know.) I studied far away, lived by myself and started to come to terms with who I was.

I took the gamble that life had to be better if I could find a place to be myself so I decided that after university I would live abroad. Years of resisting other people's opinions had given me a resilience that I never knew I had. I packed up my suitcase to fly to London with no job or accommodation in place, and I started from there. Phase Two complete.

If you have never felt oppressed in some way, I can't explain the feeling when it finally falls away. You suddenly don't have to be on alert all the time, watch everything that you say or hide who you are. Being able to be myself was like being able to exhale for the first time after holding my breath for years. It's only when you taste freedom that you can see how tight your bonds were.

I recently discovered just how toxic my upbringing was. I volunteer for a charity and last year I received training on child abuse. It was eye-opening and at times painful to see what counts as psychological and emotional abuse and what constitutes a healthy upbringing. At the same time, I had therapy for pain management and realised that my entire frame of mind was based on the shame and guilt I was made to feel for being different.

I'm still amazed I survived.

I chose to come out

I hadn't consciously planned to come out but I blurted out I had a girlfriend when my mother asked if I had a boyfriend (again). I was renting a flat in the UK, had a permanent job at the time and was in my first relationship with a woman. I had come out to most of my friends by then. My mother had a surprisingly positive reaction. She told me that she was okay with it, but I shouldn't tell my father or sister. *They* wouldn't understand, *they* were narrow-minded, not like *her*. It was our little secret. The warning signs couldn't have been bigger if they'd been flashing neon on Times Square.

I shrugged, thought it had gone well and there was no rush to come out to the rest of my family since it didn't seem to be a big deal to her and my relationship wasn't serious.

Years passed. I started a relationship with one of my friends and knew from day two she was the one (not exactly busting those lesbian stereotypes). I relocated, changed jobs and moved in with her after four months. Stupidly, I hadn't thought much about what my family would make of this.

I was on the phone with my mother when I heard her tell my sister I had moved in with a housemate for cheaper rent. She changed the subject when I asked about it. It was still to be our little secret, *they* wouldn't understand. When I announced to her that we were engaged, she had an awful reaction. My mother's pride could deal with a wayward daughter in a different country but not one who was going to get married. Months of angry and tearful phone calls followed. She started by saying they wouldn't come to the wedding and my fiancée wasn't allowed in their home. I will never forget her saying

'You can't do this to us' when talking about one of the happiest moments of my life. My father's reaction was interesting. He thought that what I was doing was 'abnormal' (*thanks*, Dad) but he still wanted me to be happy. (Highlights of that particular conversation included 'You never wore skirts', warnings about AIDS and, bizarrely, using condoms). After many months, it turned out that my father and sister were supportive (in their own way) but my mother wasn't.

They did come to our wedding. The condition was that I didn't invite any other family members (most of them probably still don't know I'm married). They met my wife five minutes before we walked down the aisle (I really, *really* don't recommend this). I always think it must have come as a bit of a shock for my mother to see so many people proud to be at my wedding and showering us with love. In the end, my parents stayed less than 24 hours and have never been back since.

To this day, my mother cannot bear to be seen in public with me and my wife. She thinks she's being subtle – and I did give her the benefit of the doubt the first few times – but she always walks a few paces behind us and will never introduce us to friends she meets on the street. There are no words to express how it feels when you know the person who brought you into this world is so deeply ashamed of you that they hide you from others – madwoman in the attic style. For years I thought the fault lay with me. I was so monstrously abnormal that I deserved only shame and disappointment. Now there are people in my life who love me and tell me that they are proud of me, as my mother never could. I often find it hard to believe them.

People who know me now are mystified by my family situation. Homophobia is so last century, isn't it? I have been estranging myself a little more every day. There are many reasons for this, some of which I've shared here. Others I don't feel ready to share yet. I always feel that in the same way I hate that they are ashamed of me for being who I am, I shouldn't be ashamed of them for being who they are. I know it isn't the same, but it sometimes feels like it. I still yearn to be the perfect daughter so much that I will take the abuse and turn the other cheek.

I know that I will never ever be their idea of a perfect daughter. And that's okay. Phase Three was a big one for me.

I chose to be myself

I found a job in an industry I love. I found my soulmate. I now read even more voraciously than when I was younger and I still don't do parties; I don't wear anything remotely sexy or feminine and strangely the world hasn't exploded. I feel so much rage now when I look back at all the ridiculous rules I was meant to respect.

It isn't easy to build up a life when your entire moral code has been warped from a very young age. I tend to overthink everything and speculate over the consequences of my actions. I have panic attacks thinking about people knowing about my life and I still fear that some parts of me need to be hidden away.

It may sound dramatic but I sometimes have to be reminded that I am *not* evil. That I do *not* deserve to hurt. That I am *not* one of the bad guys. And if my mother will not love me for who I am, there are others who will. It is still hard to hear about people having normal upbringings – though is there really any such thing? It feels alien to me that mothers can love their daughters unconditionally. It's painful to hear about 'perfect' mother-daughter relationships. A part of me will always feel like that was a failing on my part. But I am not the only person with a terrible relationship with my mother – there are lots of us out there and our voices should be heard.

Real life isn't like fiction; there are no neat and tidy endings. Now I know the words to describe my upbringing, it feels that I'm even more fucked up than I thought. Though ignorance is bliss, I always think there is a power in knowing. At the very least, the knowledge can inform all your future choices.

I know there will be many bumps in the road ahead, I know that I may not have yet gone through the worst, and I know I have many choices ahead of me. Choosing to tell my story was just one of them.

'TOUCH ME AGAIN AND I WILL FUCKING KILL YOU':
CULTURAL RESISTANCE TO GENDERED VIOLENCE IN THE PUNK ROCK COMMUNITY

Ren Aldridge

Content note: Some non-descriptive examples of sexual violence.

Every time Petrol Girls play a show I try to use the opportunity of having the mic to speak about consent; about not trying to fuck people when they're sleeping or wasted or frozen up and silent; about asking first, and making sure everyone involved in a sexual activity actually wants to do it. This is basic shit, but the countless conversations I have with women[*1] and other survivors at gigs confirm my feeling that it's something we have to keep talking about.

This essay is not a professional or academic piece of research, but my attempt to weave those conversations together with my own observations, to form my interpretation of how gendered violence operates in the punk community; and how we're fighting back. I will not go into detail or sensationalise those experiences here. Not only do I want to avoid endangering other people who have entrusted me with their stories; but it's also a political decision to move the focus away from us and on to the context that this gendered violence happens in.

I refuse to write inwards, to scrape out my personal experiences for inspection, or entertain the idea that I have to somehow

---

1   Where I put a little [*] next to 'woman', I emphasise that it's an open definition – it's up to you how you relate to that gender category.

justify my anger at what has happened to so many of us. It puts us in a defensive position, and reflects the focus in wider society and court rooms on what she/they did, what she/they wore, if she/they drank, as if this bullshit is our responsibility, instead of asking why the fuck men – because it is overwhelmingly cisgender[2] men as I will discuss later – keep doing this. I want to put this conversation on the offensive, and look at the patterns and wider context it happens in.

'Gendered violence' is a term I've taken from a zine produced by Salvage Collective. The zine was an outcome of their research on this kind of violence in activist communities and has been an invaluable resource, giving me the tools and confidence to back up my claims. Finding the words to describe what happens is sometimes half the battle. Salvage 'use the terms violence, abuse and harm to refer to a range of acts and behaviours that are described by survivors that fit on a continuum[3] of everyday harassment and intrusions to criminalised forms of sexual violence including sexual assault and rape.'[4]

The vital parts of this definition are the continuum and that the violence is described by survivors. We are the authority on our own experiences; on what happens to our own bodies. In another definition of the term Nancy Lombard writes: 'Gendered violence is rooted in the structural inequalities between men and women. It is both a cause and consequence of gender inequality.'[5]

---

2   Denoting or relating to a person whose sense of personal identity and gender corresponds with their birth sex.
3   Liz Kelly, 1998 referenced in Downes, Julia., Karis Hanson & Rebecca Hudson, *Salvage: Gendered Violence in Activist Communities*. (Leeds, UK: Footprint Workers Co-op, 2016) p. 7.
4   Ibid.
5   Lombard, Nancy, 'Gendered violence: a cause and a consequence of inequality', European Commission, www.enege.eu/sites/default/files/14-Nancy-Lombard.pdf. Accessed 29 January 2017.

Ren Aldridge

The position I'm writing from, in the context of this collection of women's* stories, is as a cisgender woman who has only experienced such violence from cisgender men. However, it is unacceptable to erase other survivors' experiences – it's important to acknowledge that anyone is capable of being an abuser or survivor. I am using these non-gender specific terms to describe the people doing (abuser) and receiving (survivor) gendered violence, except points where I want to consider this patriarchal structure and binary gender separation as the context in which the majority of gendered violence happens.

'Survivor' is a term I've personally struggled with because it makes me feel melodramatic and awkward, probably because of where I place many of my own experiences on the continuum of gendered violence. But I feel like it's important to also identify myself as a survivor here; as someone who has experienced gendered violence but doesn't like to be understood as a victim. (I also consider it to come with an optional Destiny's Child soundtrack.)

The survivors I've spoken with include people of colour but in this essay I have not explored the impact of race on experiences of sexual violence, which is a major limitation. Salvage recognise that all survivors who took part in their first research project were white and emphasise that '[t]he need for better understandings of how sexual violence intersects with race ... is paramount and [a] clear avenue for further research projects and solidarity work.'[6] Punk is noted by Salvage as one of the many groups in which survivors spoke about experiencing gendered violence,[7] and I'd place it as overlapping with the activist communities they write about.

Finishing off this theme of unstable definitions, I want to emphasise that the punk community I'm writing about is the

6   Downes, Julia. Karis Hanson & Rebecca Hudson, *Salvage: Gendered Violence in Activist Communities*. (Leeds, UK: Footprint Workers Co-op, 2016) p. 57.
7   Ibid, p. 13.

European one that I'm familiar with. A consistency worth underlining is that every part of the scene I've toured in has been completely dominated by white people, despite anti-racism being a core of punk and other radical left groups' politics.

It feels good to write openly about gendered violence for this collection of women's* stories. Speaking out about our experiences breaks the silence that maintains this violence. It is broken in bursts, snowballing once the first person tentatively speaks up. Sometimes an account of one individual's behaviour sparks further accounts from other people, exposing a pattern of serial abuse. Other times, one person's experience resonates with another's, and validates their feelings about it enough for them to speak out about a separate incident with different abusers. The silence is broken by the tiniest sounds, and their echoes can be huge.

There are, however, so many reasons why we don't speak. As survivors it is *not* our responsibility to: it's our choice how we want to deal with it. Personally, at times I've found speaking up about past incidents to be more traumatic than the incidents themselves. Investigating why can provide insight into how the culture of silence that conceals, and therefore allows continued, gendered violence is maintained; and what can be done to change that. Whilst some gendered violence may happen out of ignorance, many perpetrators rely on the silence of survivors in order to knowingly continue their behaviour unchallenged, or at least not be held accountable for past actions.

Many of us choose not to speak up because of the anticipated backlash. Salvage identify the risk of 'losing an important place of belonging and valuable social attachments,'[8] and additionally I think there's also a fear of dividing or otherwise damaging our communities. This becomes complicated within the more politicised end of punk rock that overlaps with activist groups,

---

8   Ibid, p. 31.

as its position on feminism and sexual politics claims to be ahead of the mainstream. Salvage underline: 'The persistence of and inability to deal with sexual violence contradicts the core values of equality and social justice at the heart of radical social movements.' The punk rock community prides itself on its anti-authority stance and radical (though often merely liberal) politics.

Yet, as one survivor quoted in Salvage points out: 'I think with radical circles, 9 times out of 10, it's just a microcosm of what already exists, just with different haircuts.' Activist and punk circles claim to counter mainstream society whilst reproducing the exact same power dynamics, focusing their efforts outside whilst not considering what's happening inside. Salvage reflect that 'many survivors talked about implicit hierarchies which individuals used to exert power in activism. This often replicated power hierarchies of wider society that privileged older, white, middle class, able-bodied and cisgender men.'[9]

I asked Diana Muertos from the Love Sex, Hate Sexism collective if she saw such hierarchies playing out within punk rock and if so how:

> *It's crazy, I thought I got into punk because there was no hierarchy but it totally is the most hierarchical sub-group or social group I have ever come across. It's just like you can do whatever the fuck you want if you're in a band, you totally get protected, and there's even this kind of mentality that you can just go on tour and get laid and do what you want and leave town the next day and there isn't accountability for that, and there's this disbelief of anyone who says different. It is quite a protection racket I think. People are just so, so loyal to a band.*

It's definitely worth considering this unquestioning loyalty towards bands. Part of it, sure, is a sense of belonging to a

---

9   Ibid, p. 33.

community, but there's also something to be said for the value that we place on music and the resulting overblown status of musicians. Music creates an emotional response. When someone's songs speak to you, and validate your feelings about the world, it's natural to feel a connection toward the person that wrote them. It can be painful and bitterly disappointing to find out that a musician you respect is an abuser. It completely alters the way you feel about the music that meant so much to you and I think it's fair to acknowledge that it hurts.

The problem lies with where we direct our hurt and anger; so often towards those exposing gendered violence. This carries a worrying implication that someone's creative output gives them more worth or legitimacy than a survivor, or more sinister still, that this creative output is in itself somehow more important than the lived experience of survivors. This is echoed in activist communities where the safety of survivors can be deemed less important than 'the cause.' Even in more outwardly feminist parts of the punk community, disproportionate allowance is still given to those in bands.

If an unknown within the community, perhaps a random guy in the crowd, is touching people up, it's easy for everyone to unanimously condemn such behaviour. When it's someone visible, like someone in a band or promoter, the issue suddenly becomes much more divisive. I feel like this is because we protect our friends and a challenge on our friend's behaviour feels like a challenge to our belief that our friends are fundamentally 'good' people.

When I took a friend who had sexually assaulted me through an accountability process in early 2016, the hardest part was getting him to admit to it being sexual assault. He couldn't accept that he was capable of doing something like that, whilst holding his political beliefs, and being a 'good person'. He didn't even try to deny what had happened; he just couldn't describe it in those words. We left it at 'Yeah, it is what you say it is, and I'm sorry and I'll never do this to anyone again' which will just have to be good enough. It was as though admitting to it would alter his entire identity, and render his political beliefs as somehow untrue. As Julia Downes writes: 'to be accused of harm threatens the foundations of our identities.'[10]

It made me think about the way that I couldn't understand some of the other things that happened to me as sexual assault because of the way that I perceived the men who did it as 'good' people. It's as though this idea of 'good' and 'bad' people raises the stakes so that there isn't any room for meaningful accountability; you're either good and innocent or bad and guilty. Salvage also identified a binary in terms of trust – one survivor describing it as 'very black and white sometimes. You're either in and [...] trusted or [...] out and you'll never be trusted again.'[11] Perhaps stakes are higher in activist communities where people are participating in illegal direct actions together, but the whole punk community has a looser version of the same culture of distrust. I knew that if I spoke up about the friend I mentioned above, that our part of the punk community would split. And it did. We all lost out as a result.

These binaries, these needs to define things as one or the other, leave no space for possibility or change. The definition of gendered violence as a continuum[12] validated a shift in my understanding of it. As part of my feminist activism, I've been arguing *hard* against the idea of a 'grey area' on issues of rape

10 Downes, Julia. 'Six key messages about sexual violence in UK activist communities', Open Democracy, 27 January 2016. www.opendemocracy.net/transformation/julia-downes/salvaging-listening-to-sexual-violence-survivors-in-uk-activist-communit.
11 Downes, Julia. Karis Hanson & Rebecca Hudson, *Salvage: Gendered Violence in Activist Communities*. (Leeds, UK: Footprint Workers Co-op, 2016), p. 33.
12 Downes, Julia. Karis Hanson & Rebecca Hudson, Salvage: Gendered Violence in Activist Communities. (Leeds, UK: Footprint Workers Co-op, 2016), p. 7.

and sexual violence for years. I stand by that activism, because this 'grey area' is used against survivors time and time again. Arguments such as 'It wasn't proper rape' remain disgusting; non-consensual penetration remains rape; and non-consensual sexual touching remains sexual assault. However, I think that understanding gendered violence as a continuum, that ranges from 'everyday harassment and intrusions to criminalised forms of sexual violence including sexual assault and rape'[13] might be key to holding people meaningfully accountable.

What needs to be fought for, is survivors' rights to define and position our own experiences on this continuum. I understand my own experiences in this way, even within those I define as sexual assault, with some assaults far more sinister and deliberate than others. This massively affects how I feel I want to deal with things, and in some instances, I haven't wanted to say anything for fear of the pro-survivor side of a binary outcome: he has sexually assaulted me, therefore he is a bad guy and must be kicked out the community. Most of the time I just wanted them to recognise their behaviour for what it was and not to do it again, to anyone. There is the added aspect here of calling out as caring, in that if someone I care about fucks up, I expect better of them and I want them to rectify their behaviour.

Our whole cultural perception of sexism, as the context in which the majority of gendered violence happens, seems to be understood in the same binary terms. We say 'you are sexist' not 'what you've done is sexist.' It's as though sexism is some inherent quality that you either are or are not, rather than this whole structure or culture that we're socialised into, and that we are all capable of perpetuating. Actually, we seem to view most isms and phobias this way. Just because I'm a woman* who identifies as a feminist, does not mean I am incapable of perpetuating it, or the sexist culture that it happens in. We are all complicit here. The fact that gendered violence is

---

13   Ibid

overwhelmingly enacted by men on women[*] is not because women[*] are incapable of fucking up; a lot of it's because we're not brought up to feel that we're entitled to other people's bodies. Sometimes we barely feel entitled to our own. There is an endless amount to consider about the damaging way in which we're socialised into a sexist culture which separates us into limited binary gender categories.

Binaries. Good guys and nasty women. Brave heroes and wicked witches. Strong boys and pretty girls. From the moment we pop out the womb and get announced as boy or girl. It's all so fucking fairytale, and this is hugely significant. Every culture's stories reflect and produce its values. Culture is basically a constantly developing expression of our values. Rape culture is an increasingly understood term that describes 'cultural practices that excuse or otherwise tolerate sexual violence.'[14] It's the culture that gendered violence happens in. Girls Against, a campaign group challenging sexual harassment at punk shows state that 'sexual harassment happens because of complex attitudes which are installed in our culture.'[15] Salvage underline a need to 'open up and question cultural norms, values and power hierarchies that allow and sustain sexual violence.'[16] Culture comes up again and again. To stop gendered violence happening, we need to change the culture it happens in.

A key way that we are already doing this, is through our own expressions of culture; through music, art, campaigns and

14   Ridgway, Shannon. '25 Everyday Examples of Rape Culture', Everyday Feminism, 10 March 2014, www.everydayfeminism.com/2014/03/examples-of-rape-culture/.
15   'Frequently Asked Questions/Common Concerns', Girls Against, www.girlsagainst.tumblr.com/faq. Accessed 29 January 2017.
16   Downes, Julia. Karis Hanson & Rebecca Hudson, *Salvage: Gendered Violence in Activist Communities*. (Leeds, UK: Footprint Workers Co-op, 2016), p. 60.

writing. Making rape culture and wider structures enabling gendered violence audible and visible, makes such structures tangible and easier to break. War On Women's song 'Say It' is a perfect example of direct resistance, with lyrics that explicitly dissect rape culture – 'What if I was 30 or 12? What if I had one drink?' – and that counter the culture of silencing: 'Say it! Say it! I was raped!' The music video begins with a helpline for survivors, and collaborates with The Monument Quilt Project; an ongoing art project where survivors continually add quilt squares as a means of expression. This can be both healing for survivors to place their experiences among others, and serve to expose how widespread the issue is.

Punk culture is also resisting in visual ways, from toilet graffiti to full campaigns with posters and merch. Graffiti, like the massive 'Nein heißt nein' painted on the wall of Rote Flora in Hamburg, exists in DIY spaces across Europe. Girl Gangs Over Graz pasted life-size cut-outs of masked up women* all over Graz, as well as inside the local DIY venue. The cut-outs include feminist slogans in German and English such as 'I never ask for it, not with my clothing, not with my behaviour.'[17] By placing cut-outs inside the gig space as well as outside, it acknowledges that the same sexist shit can still happen within the punk community. This challenges the in/out trust binary described above by survivors in Salvage's research.

Flyering is another tactic (useful in commercial spaces that are less tolerant of feminist graffiti being pasted or sprayed on interior walls). This was an obvious choice for Love Sex, Hate Sexism: 'We're punk rockers, we're gonna make flyers,'[18] explained Diana, who began the collective with a group friends to deal with a sexual assault in their friendship circle. By using a visual language familiar to that community (i.e. punk as fuck) LSHS is a far more legitimate and effective way of educating

17   *Girl Gangz Over Graz*, www.girlgangsovergraz.wordpress.com/. Accessed 03 February 2017.
18   Phone interview with Diana Muertos in December 2016.

our community about consent than any official, governmental or police campaign ever could be.

A broader, less punk-specific campaign is Good Night Out, whose posters are an increasingly common sight across the UK. The campaign encourages venues to train their staff and display posters stating their Pledge: 'We want you to have a good night out. If something or someone makes you feel uncomfortable, no matter how minor it may seem, you can report it to any member of staff and they will work with you to make sure it doesn't have to ruin your night.'[19] These posters are directed at people who receive harassment, taking the pressure off them to do something about it, with the venue staff taking responsibility.

Similarly, DIY Space For London have an accountability agreement on posters displayed around the space. This agreement also offers help from volunteers running the space, whilst addressing everyone using it. These two examples are the broadest I've come across in terms of addressing the full continuum of gendered violence. They don't try to prescribe what sexual harassment, assault or any other form of gendered violence is, but leave it open to the survivor to define their own experience.

Alongside these direct strategies of resistance, the changing gender balance amongst those active in the punk community is also having an impact. More and more women*, trans and non-gender-conforming people are putting on shows and playing in bands. Whilst songs and visual campaigns expose oppressive structures, the changing gender dynamic means that the people most affected by them are becoming more visible. The more of us on stage, the more we can talk, sing and shout about our own experiences. We've been doing this since the birth of punk, and whilst we've always been a minority, it's

---

19   'About Us', Good Night Out Campaign, www.goodnightoutcampaign.org/about/. Accessed 03 February 2017.

changing. Hierarchies that protect those in bands may well still exist, but it's increasingly less dominated by cis men. We don't need them to create the music and put on the gigs that our community thrives on. The less dependent we are, the less tolerant the community might be of shit behaviour. And whilst it shouldn't give anyone's argument any weight, it's still pretty satisfying to respond to 'But he plays in a political band' with 'Yeah, so do I.'

I recognise that because of my band, I've moved up the punk community's bullshit hierarchy. It's an uncomfortable recognition but things have changed a lot for me. I definitely feel the protection that comes with being in a band. As a woman* I feel like I receive a lot less gendered violence. I'm not saying it never happens any more, but hey, no-one's touched me up during a tour in years. Screaming 'Touch me again and I'll fucking kill you' down the mic on a regular basis probably helps. But it's also to do with being visible and being listened to. And that's fucked up. Of course I'm relieved that I feel safer, but feeling safe shouldn't depend on climbing a hierarchy. As women*, trans and non-binary people, we need to keep infecting that hierarchy, exposing it and tearing it down.

There's massive catharsis in having the mic, and being able to use the stage as an opportunity to talk about consent. I remember a several times when the band was in its earlier stages, when I got to speak into crowds containing men that had assaulted me or my friends. It felt incredible: a reversal of power, however momentary. I love hardcore punk and heavy music because I love releasing the aggression. I feel like I'm taking the violence that surrounds me and spewing it back out, releasing all the weird feelings that normally chew up my insides outwards, loudly.

But I'm also exhausted. And the catharsis that came initially with speaking up is wearing off. I still talk to survivors at shows regularly, and I value the sense of sisterhood that comes with those conversations, but I'm burning out. To echo what I wrote at the start of this essay: every time Petrol Girls play a show I try to use the opportunity of having the mic to speak about consent. I feel like I'm stuck talking about it. I don't want to anymore. I'm sick of explaining it. There are a thousand other things I want to talk about. There are other political issues I want to pour more energy into. I want to be part of meaningfully opposing the rise in far right and fascist politics. I want to fight for freedom of movement and stand in solidarity with refugees and migrants and I'm furious that so much of my energy is taken up with trying to make the community that I need as a base and means of support safe. This is a whole community problem. The last group of people whose responsibility it is to solve it is survivors. None of this was our fault.

ON NAMING

Nadine Aisha Jassat

'America ties a horse to each corner of my name, and pulls… America wants my name to not exist.' – Fatimah Asghar[1]

'My name doesn't allow me to trust anyone that cannot pronounce it right.' – Warsan Shire[2]

It's 10pm, late, and there's a pull on my Twitter handle. A man, nameless to me, is responding to recent Tweets I sent about the work the Rape Crisis movement are doing in Scotland. *An unfortunate name to be highlighting Rape Crisis*, he says. It takes a beat before I realise he means me. I scroll his profile – full of Tweets preaching hatred for Islam, claiming that rape is only ever committed by Muslim and migrant men. I'm tempted to tell him I work for Rape Crisis in Scotland; that my entire career has been in Scotland's violence against women sector. I'm tempted to send him the UK criminal justice statistics which show, overwhelmingly, perpetrators of sexual offences are white British men.[3] Instead, as my key hovers over the block button, I picture him sat at an unseen desk in an unknown city

---

1   Asghar, Fatimah. 'Fatimah Ashghar's Poem', TWCorg's channel, *You-Tube*, 15 September 2015. www.youtube.com/watch?v=b8Vf-6zs-S0
2   Rasheed, Kameelah Janan. 'To Be Vulnerable and Fearless: An Interview with Writer Warsan Shire', *The Well & Often Reader*, November 2012. www.wellandoftenpress.com/reader/to-be-vulnerable-and-fear-less-an-interview-with-writer-warsan-shire/.
3   'Are Asians disproportionately represented in prosecutions for sex offences?', *Full Fact*, 10 May 2012. www.fullfact.org/news/are-asians-dis-proportionately-represented-prosecutions-sex-offences/.

typing, grabbing my name, seizing the full ocean flow of it, drawing my Muslim British African Indian self as it follows the @ key. Tag, you're it.

It's 8pm, on a train somewhere between Edinburgh and Glasgow, and I'm getting tired. I stare out through the window, knowing Scotland hurries past me in the darkness outside, but seeing only my own reflection in the rushing lights which shine on toughened glass. I'm thinking about all the times I've told someone my name – restaurant bookings, doctor's appointments, agency calls at work – to have them ask me repeat it before they say 'Oh, you mean-----' and present me with a mispronounced version of myself, a word that is not mine but which, for a quiet life, I answer to. I'm thinking about the small disappointment which nestles now in my ribs – which I wish I didn't have, but I do – as I realise that at not one of the five events I have spoken at in the past week did I hear my name pronounced correctly. I think of the flinch I try to hide from my face as I am introduced to the audience with a name which is mine but not mine; a name I do not say. I scold myself that I am not one to complain, that I surely mispronounce others' names too, whilst a deeper part of me realises that I don't think there's ever been an event where I have heard my full name pronounced properly. I soothe myself with the lullaby that I must just not be able to remember.

I do remember being six, in a moment which years later will become a heartbroken family joke. We are returning from visiting my father's family, my family. The immigration officer at London Heathrow holds my mother's passport in his hands, and looks at the list of names on there – mine, hers, my brother's. My father's passport is forest green; he stands in another queue. The officer bends down, looks at me, sees dark hair, dark eyes, pale brown skin. Looks at my mother, sees white with a 90s perm. He says to me: 'What's your name little girl?' looking between me, my mother, and the words stamped on her passport. I do not reply, stare at his hands and look for my reflection in the gleam of gold and red. I never have responded well to white men in suits asking me to explain myself. My mother's hand is warm in mine as she says: 'Go on Nadine, tell him your name'.

My name is Nadine Aisha Jassat. At the time of writing I am, according to a database of historical and genealogical records, the only Jassat in Scotland, and one of less than 200 in the UK.[4] I joke that when I pass my name on to my children this means we can start a Jassat clan. I have lost count of the times I have been called Nadia, even when stood next to a board with my name written on it. My middle name, Aisha, is after my paternal grandmother's sister; I hear I would have liked her, but she died shortly before I was born. My first name Nadine, not pronounced the British way, isn't traditionally Muslim in contrast to my brothers. Nadine came at my mother's insistence: simply, she wanted to give her daughter a name that she loved, and Nadine was it. I've stopped hearing the mispronunciation of my first name. I cringe at the repeated mispronunciation of Aisha. I am bemused at the many variations I hear of Jassat. I know it seems a small thing to some, until you are introduced again and again as a mumbled version of yourself, each word offkey. And in the end it all adds up to a man, whose name I do not know, thinking he knows mine, sat at unseen keyboard in an unknown city, saying my name is unfortunate for the work that I do.

At least, in a way, he sees its significance – in his racism and Islamophobia he, at least, could never hold his hands up like an apologetic hipster and say that he is 'colour blind'. He sees a woman of colour, a woman with a Muslim name, writing about feminism and gender-based violence and knows that that has to mean something. Even if to him, the something it means is skewed backwards and wrong, a reason to try and silence me, to invalidate my place in my own movement. I won't tell him that

---

4   'Jassat Surname Meaning & Statistics', *Forebears*, www.forebears.io/surnames/jassat. Accessed 29 January 2017.

the worst violence ever done to me has been done by white men. I won't tell him about the shine on the face of a child in a class I taught who realised that finally, perhaps for the first time, there was a teacher in their class who looked like them and was speaking about issues which affected them, using language familiar to them. These are the truths which I live by, and yet in these instances – when my name is called into question – I need to know that the community within which I work and thrive has my back. But, as Warsan Shire points out, that is hard to do when many of them mispronounce my name.

When the community you live in will not correctly pronounce your name, and when the agents of racism, xenophobia and Islamophobia in wider society target your name, it places you in a curious position between your identity being erased and your identity being the point upon which people will attack you. For me to ask you to correctly pronounce my name is a political act: by doing so I am refusing to accept a lesser version, refusing to compromise on the notion that I and my identity matter. For mispronunciation is Othering; it exists in a context of us feeling that we have to bend, change, shape or erase ourselves to fit in. The wilful mispronunciation of mine and other's names, the attempt to not even try because it looks too 'difficult', too long (ultimately and often unsaid *too foreign*), is an act of Othering which exists in and reinforces a wider context of racism and white supremacy. I am reminded of the experience of Uzoamaka Aduba, who recalls coming home from school asking to be called 'Zoe' as nobody knew how to pronounce Uzoamaka. To which her mother replied: 'If they can learn to say Tchaikovsky and Michelangelo and Dostoyevsky, they can learn to say Uzoamaka'.[5]

---

5   Nigatu, Heben. '"Orange Is The New Black: Star Uzo Aduba On Why She Wouldn't Change Her Nigerian Name', *BuzzFeed*, 24 June 2014. www.buzzfeed.com/hnigatu/orange-is-the-new-black-star-uzo-aduba-on-why-she-wouldnt-ch?utm_term=.oiBwepQmM#.lqO80X-yDz..

To live in a culture which will grow your tongue so that some names will roll from it, but others will not, reveals much about who and what said culture values. That children are taught to pronounce the name of a composer whose work they may not even know, but do not say the name of the girl who sits across from them every day in class, is a tool of cultural imperialism. It is a clear line, a line heavy with empire and white supremacy, which says: *these are the people who are of worth, whose names you need to remember, who you need to respect, and these are the people who can remain nameless, who you don't need to respect, who are alien to you.*

The dehumanisation present here is the first step in justifying violence, of saying you don't belong, you matter less, and we can do what we like to you. It is not an accident that studies have revealed racist profiling made by employers, who when shortlisting applications make choices based on stereotypical and racist interpretations of candidates' names.[6] John Smith would sail through; Nadine Aisha Jassat, not so much. It is not a coincidence that, at the same time we saw an increase in Islamophobic rhetoric in the media and public eye, that reports of Islamophobic hate crimes rose by over 300% in a single year; the majority carried out by young white men against Muslim women.[7] This, on naming, is real life, is as structural as it is everyday. Even now as I write at my computer, a red line zigzags under Uzoamaka, whilst Tchaikovsky goes unchecked. A subtle reminder, programmed in, of who the system works for and who is out of place.

---

6   Howard, Jacqueline. 'New Study Confirms Depressing Truth About Names And Racial Bias', *The Huffington Post*, 10 August 2015. www.huffingtonpost.com/entry/black-sounding-names-study_us_561697a5e4b0dbb8000d687f.

7   Sherwood, Harriet. 'Incidents of Anti-Muslim Abuse up by 326% in 2015, says Tell Mama', *The Independent*, 29 June 2016. www.theguardian.com/society/2016/jun/29/incidents-of-anti-muslim-abuse-up-by-326-in-2015-says-tell-mama.

On Naming

How you respond to my name can be my first measure of how you will respond to me as a person. Will you deny my existence, or will you fight to support its validity? You could say that I could tell it all by your commitment to correctly pronouncing my name. I'm not saying that mispronunciation can't happen genuinely – it certainly can and does – but we need to talk about how it can also be deliberate, a repetition echoing like the clang of a hammer through history, pushing you down, pushing you *out*. We need to recognise where it sits within the wider context. When someone continues to mispronounce my name, even after hearing me say it multiple times, or when I sit – like I did on that Scottish train – and realise I never hear my name spoken the way it is meant to be, it sends a clear message of erasure to me, a sense of being wilfully unseen. It denies the recognition that my name exists, that I exist in all my multi-layered and mixed identities. My name spans continents, in it as in me are multiple cultures, faiths, and ethnicities, coexisting and thriving in one. My name carries my heritage and is at the same time the future that I aspire to. Making no effort to pronounce that future correctly delays the speed at which it will come to be. Just as words have power, just as magic spells are always a combination of letters and syllables, and just as we have known since childhood that all we need is the magic word to unlock the door, so too do names and naming hold power.

Social justice movements have long recognised the power of language, and what words are chosen to describe who. A woman is 'bossy' where a man is 'ambitious.' A black or brown man is a 'terrorist'; a white man 'mentally unstable'. In my work within the movement to end violence against women, we are familiar with this term 'nasty woman', and its sisters *slut, bitch,* and *man-hater.* We know what it is to be the bogeywoman. And for those of us who cross multiple strands, the threat we pose to the white patriarchal status quo, and the danger we face from it, draws on multiple strands of our identity that cannot be separated. *Paki bitch. Angry black woman.* Just as I was seen as a 'nasty woman' by the Islamophobe on Twitter for my connection to Islam, so too have I been seen as a nasty woman in my work in the movement to end violence against women. 'Feminist' gets misrepresented as a a dirty word, echoing throughout the timeline of experiences of activists in the women's movement since the 70s and longer; we've been seen as the radical feminists who want women to leave their husbands, become lesbians, dye their hair green. If wanting a woman to be able to own her own sexuality, to be able to live life with freedom and dignity and find and make her own choices are these things, then yes, we are nasty women – the nastiest around.

We must not forget that the names we are called matter: they define how we sit within a society, and what we need to disrupt in order to exist. When someone enquires after my ethnicity and asks '*What* are you?' they tell me much about how far we have to go to dismantle the dehumanising effect of white supremacy. When someone hears me say my name Nadine, but looks at my face and sees Nadia, it tells me how far I still have to push to be recognised as a mixed heritage woman, all strands seen, rather than the one which the viewer feels is the closest fit.

It's the reason I love Fatimah Asghar's poem 'Fatimah', quoted at the start of this piece, so much. Her poem begins: 'America's got no keychain for my name' – and I am back, I am 6, and 10, and 12, searching for my name in tacky shops in tourist seaside towns.[8] They don't make an Aisha keychain in the UK because they don't want to acknowledge we exist; accuse us, Muslim women, of not doing enough to 'integrate' whilst simultaneously upholding and maintaining structures that make us invisible. So I carry my name as proof of survival. It holds the women I carry with me: Aisha, for who I was named and with whom I apparently share a cheeky sense of

---

8   Asghar, Fatimah. 'Fatimah Ashghar's Poem', TWCorg's channel, *You-Tube*, 15 September 2015. www.youtube.com/watch?v=b8Vf-6zs-S0&-feature=youtu.be.

humour and a love of beautiful things, and my mother who fought for this name Nadine.

At a lecture given by Nawal El Saadawi in Edinburgh in 2015, I heard her say that for a woman to give her name to her child is a defining step in the ending of patriarchal rule, for instead of submitting to the name of the father we honour and own and recognise the name of the mother.[9] Because, essentially, it sets out who has more power – whose narrative and heritage is deemed to be more important, and whose can get forgotten and discarded at the wayside of history. Patriarchy is built, Nawal El Saadawi tells us, on 'ignoring the name of the mother' – so to dismantle it we must honour that name instead. It is precisely the reason why any suggestion that I would change my name, not pass on my name to my children, feels like an insult. Imagine were I to have children with a white British man, a son of empire, and to have my name removed and replaced with his simply because he is a man. Is there not an imperialism here based on both misogyny and racism? Is there not a violence which has a lingering taste of colonisation and male power?

The Jassat name has survived centuries of migration; it could have begun in India with Jasset, Jasat, or more. I have cousins whose surnames are different from their siblings because, during apartheid and Zimbabwe's 'colour bar', the white British registrars didn't really care whether the father's name Yusuf was a first name or a surname, didn't care if it was spelt with a Y or an E. Our names tell histories, and my cousin's names – a word that sounds like a blurred version of Yusuf but does not resemble it on paper – tell of the deliberate attempts at erasure of that history, and of the something new which was born out of adapting to survive. By writing this piece in the here and now, by telling this story, by passing on my name, I am telling of

9   Thursday 12 March 2015, Edinburgh University. Podcast recording available courtesy of the Alwaleed centre online via: www.casaw.ac.uk/events-2/casaw-events/. Specific section from 42 minutes in.

our survival. By asking you to pronounce my name correctly, I am showing the respect I have for it, and my understanding of the history through which it has had to survive.

So how did I respond to the Twitter troll, to the one who grabbed my name? The day after I went into my work, my job which challenges gender-based violence, opened my email inbox, clicked on the setting for my signature. And I saw my short name, the two thirds of it: *Nadine Jassat*. I pressed down five keys with satisfaction. A-I-S-H-A. I already know in my work how much representation matters; I know because I see my own reflection in the faces of children when they see me standing at the front of their classroom. I know because the ones who look like me tell me they remember me, even years later. I look at my signature and sigh, enjoy the full sight of it next to the name of my organisation making clear who I am, what I do, and what I stand for. I feel a certainty that I will not accept anything less going ahead. People need to know who they are dealing with.

LAURA JANE GRACE:
NAMING, SPEAKING OUT
AND THE SUBVERSION OF ART
IN CONVERSATION WITH SASHA DE BUYL-PISCO

Laura Jane Grace is a real rock star. This goes deeper than the tour bus, the rock star cred, the look. Music is simply a part of her. Even though her work is punk rock, full of grimy chords and powerful emotion, when she plays, she is full of joy.

Making music has been a part of Grace's life since she was very young and though she first started playing in church talent shows, her music has long eschewed convention. Her band, Against Me!, were formed when Laura was seventeen, and have seen her through some of the toughest times in her life, including her choice to come out as trans and begin a very public transition in May 2012. As an established musician, coming out quietly wasn't an option for her. Instead, she told the world in a *Rolling Stone* feature, and has maintained an incredible honesty about her transition and its impact on her personal and family life since then.

'Well, you know, in a way I didn't have the luxury of not, doing what I do,' she notes when we sit down to talk. 'It's not like I came out as trans and then started a band and then like all of a sudden was going on tour. I've been in a band for twenty years.'

Today she uses her status as a rock icon to help raise awareness of trans issues, reaching people who might never have even heard the word 'trans,' thanks to Against Me!'s loyal following. 'I recognise there's a platform and I'm happy to use that in a way to raise visibility, but at the same time, sometimes, the pressure is a little overwhelming, to be honest.'

She's aware that given her position, people often expect her to speak on behalf of all trans people, and she is careful not to overstep. Of being a spokesperson, she says, 'I just try to speak for myself and I try to give that forewarning too. All I can really do is speak for myself and my experiences.'

We speak a little bit about how today's political climate has impacted her, and she calls the reclamation of the phrase 'nasty woman' 'a pretty glorious thing'. Reclamation of words is something she is no stranger to. Her memoir *Tranny* isn't a reclamation of the term, exactly, but instead a way to take the word from others. I'm surprised to learn that the word 'tranny' is not a word Grace enjoys using.

'I don't like that word,' she notes, 'I don't want to identify with that word. I don't like to hear people being called that word, but at the same time my book is about self-hate, and internalised transphobia, so it was a fitting title.'

Grace had braced herself against the word, as if, by using it first, she could take away the ability for it to be used against her. '[Tranny] was definitely a word that I had prepared myself for. How would I react the first time I heard it?' However, when the moment finally came, Grace was shocked when it was another trans person who used the word to refer to her. She says 'it kind of took me aback for a second'. Becoming part of the trans community has led to Grace learning more about the origins of the trans movement, and words like 'tranny' form part of that.

'[It's] a really complicated word. I recently did a panel with Kate Bornstein, who is a trans writer, and she's an older generation of trans people. [She] has no problem with that word and uses the word freely in reference to herself. When I was talking to her she explained to me that the word came from trans people – Australian trans people specifically; they have a tendency to shorten every word like that – "barbecue" becomes "barbie," right?' She notes, 'I don't really see how I can argue with that. How can you tell an older generation trans person that they all of a sudden aren't allowed to use a word they've been using their whole life? I respect that.' It's almost an internal language that she hadn't learned yet, as she wasn't yet part of the community, and it's something she herself has tackled in her own music.

In Against Me!'s album *Transgender Dysphoria Blues*, she uses the word 'faggot' in the track 'Talking Transgender Dysphoria Blues'. Working through the song with her bandmates (pre-transition and pre-coming out), they questioned the lines '*They just see a faggot. They'll hold their breath not to catch the sick,*' asking 'Is that cool? Can we say that?' This was a key moment, as Grace used this a way to begin the conversation that led to her coming out to them. In the end, Grace came out and the lyrics stayed in the song. 'Context is important,' she notes.

As a musician, Grace has a vessel to really speak for herself and her own experiences. Her two most recent albums, *Shape Shift With Me* and *Transgender Dysphoria Blues,* have dealt overtly with the subject of her transition ('Boyfriend' is particularly excellent) but every piece of songwriting prior to this touches on Grace's gender dysphoria with varying degrees of subtlety.

'With music, it has the benefit of, like, even if you are really direct in a song, people tend to adapt their own meaning [from it].' This gave Grace a valuable space to work out her feelings towards herself and her body, in a context where no one would really examine it or in some cases even realise. This calls to mind the closing track on *New Wave*, Against Me!'s third studio album. Called 'The Ocean' the song is quiet and melancholy with a rhythm that resembles a marching song, but the lyrics are almost shockingly overt when you consider them within the context of Grace's transition.

'That song, in a lot of ways, is just stream of consciousness. It was all written in one sitting. [It] all just flowed out. Prior to that every Against Me! record has songs that are just me dealing with my dysphoria – dealing with whatever was going on in my head – but in the past I definitely felt like I had to mask things in metaphor or change words around. As the band progressed, I got more bold, either consciously or subconsciously, pushing myself forward and that song just has no metaphor in it whatsoever.' The lyrics go:

> *If I could have chosen, I would have been born a woman,*
> *My mother once told me, she would have named me Laura*

'There's no hidden meaning to that, it's just right there on the surface.'

Before coming out, Laura dealt with her dysphoria and depression by acting in out in very traditionally masculine 'rock star' ways. Her memoir is peppered with stories of drugs, sex, rock star fights and more, so I'm interested to ask whether the reaction to her output has changed in recent years. Has she begun to experience any gender bias after releasing work into the world as a woman?

'I feel like I'm aware of biases and things like that on multiple levels,' she says, 'and it's really complex, you know. I guess that's intersection. As a writer, I feel like I noticed, doing the book tour in the last month, that immediately there was a bias even just based on that fact that I'm most commonly known as a musician. People would assume "You're a musician, you couldn't have possibly written this book yourself. You had a ghost-writer or something". And it's like, no! I mean, I had my friend help me with it, but I wrote it! So there's that immediate bias, and then as a trans person I feel like sometimes, in certain situations, you're clocked as being mentally unstable or […] you're viewed as crazy.'

Grace possesses an impressive self-awareness and understanding of her own emotional landscape, so I'm surprised anyone could think of her as crazy. Though she faces many levels of bias on a daily basis, she's quick to speak about the positives of her experience. 'In many ways I'm really thankful for having the broader perspective of being able to see things in different ways.'

Her compassionate and complex approach has meant that, even faced with the changing nature of her work, she's managed to find connection to an audience that appreciate her politics, regardless of the genre she is working in. On her music, she says: 'I don't really see it in the confines of punk anymore. Having gone through the ringer over the years as a band... I know what punk means to me and the influence it's had on me. If someone wants to say we're punk, that's cool. If someone wants to say we're not, whatever. It doesn't fucking matter.' What remains is a steadfast desire to have her music say something. 'I think it's really important for there to be a message to the music. The music that's always mattered to me has always been intelligent. There's got to be a good melody you know, but it has to be saying something. Otherwise, what is it?'

Melody is a compelling thing, and Grace understands that music is a powerful tool, when put in the right (or wrong) hands. 'It's subversion! You have the ability to be subversive and you don't even have to be overt about it and that's not just even music, that's just art in general! I was reading something earlier that was breaking down the new *Time* magazine cover with Donald Trump on it for 'Person of the Year', and how subversive it is on multiple levels; from the M being devil horns, to the seated position, the chair, the way it was shot, and all the references there. [There are] so many levels to it.'

It seems that subversion through art will become increasingly important in a Trump era context, where people who challenge the status quo will struggle to have their voices heard. 'I think it's really important to speak out. You know, it's actually really been troubling me a lot lately and I've been spending a lot of time thinking about it. The scary thing is that the more people will speak out against Trump (seeing that he's so reactionary and will target single individuals via Twitter) the more that you're going to see more of that as his administration progresses. So, voices of dissent will be attacked and that's evidence of what type of ruler he is or what type of government it is and what is happening. I guess the hope is [that] there's power in numbers and that if everyone's speaking out then it [will be] harder to silence everything.'

The refusal to be silenced may seem like nothing, but to some, especially those in marginalised groups, it can be the hardest thing in the world. Is there anything Grace would say to people about how to get through the next few years? 'I wish I had this secret answer!' she laughs. 'I guess you look for strength within each other, you know. No one can do this alone and now more than ever we need each other.'

ADVENTURES OF A HALF-BLACK YANK IN AMERICA

Elise Hines

Leaving the Melting Pot for a Snow Globe

Growing up in New York City sheltered me from the true depth of racism in America. Queens, where I was born and raised, was hailed as one of the most diverse places on earth (statistically speaking) in the New York Daily News back in 2009.[1] As a light-skinned, biracial girl with an Anglo name from a middle-class family, I only had a handful of brushes with overt racism until I left New York for university in rural Pennsylvania.

My stint as an undergraduate at Penn State started in January of 1997. After my parents helped me unpack, and left me in the middle of nowhere before spring semester started, I did not lay eyes on another person of colour for three whole days. After making it through 19 years of life on Earth immersed in its melting pot, going three days without seeing another non-white person was jarring.

It failed to dawn on me that I was in a brand new world until I strolled down to the local grocery store. Within minutes, I was followed from aisle to aisle, by a white staff member who was conveniently tidying up whilst hot on my tail. Being from THE BIG CITY, I instinctively assumed this person was mentally unstable. Anyone who experienced the NYC subway system in the wee hours could draw the same conclusion. I didn't realise that my skin colour was the impetus for the tail until it happened again a few days later.

1   'Queens one of 'most diverse places on Earth,' new figures show' *New York Daily News*, 12 July 2009. www.nydailynews.com/new-york/ queens/queens-diverse-places-earth-new-figures-show-article-1.430744.

Adventures of a Half-Black Yank in America

Before the end of my first semester, I was followed around half the stores in downtown State College, had my backpack searched while exiting one store as a handful of young white students with unsearched backpacks passed by and stared. My hair was touched, without permission, more than a dozen times by white, female students in bathrooms (usually accompanied by a flurry of questions or compliments). I lost count of how many times I found myself at the receiving end of the, 'What exactly *are* you?' question by white students from rural Pennsylvania (i.e., Pennsyltucky[2]). It was unnerving and I started to question my decision to attend Penn State.

Since my major was not Sociology, Women's Studies, or Psychology, and the Google-less internet of 1997 was a series of text-based Bulletin Board Systems (BBS), static websites, and a smattering of webcomics, the term 'microaggression' was not part of my lexicon. When I first heard microaggression used in context, about a decade later, I'm sure the people in my immediate vicinity saw my eyes light up and heard the *thunk* of my synapses firing as I wrapped my brain around the horror of my undergraduate experience in Pennsylvania.

On the upside, while I survived the trauma (mostly psychological and emotional) of life outside of the melting pot, I met other marginalised students who educated me on how to stay safe and effectively handle racists of all magnitudes. They informed me of Pennsylvania's Black Church burnings in 1991, 1994, and 1995,[3] which tragically never made it on my radar before I enrolled. They urged me not to travel alone too far from campus at night. They told me that Fraternity Row

---

2   Slang portmanteau of state names Pennsylvania and Kentucky.
3   'Hearing before the committee on the judiciary United States senate, one hundred fourth congress, second session on the federal response to recent incidents of church burnings in predominantly black churches across the south', *U.S. Government Printing Office*, Washington, 1997. www.justice.gov/sites/default/files/jmd/legacy/2013/11/08/hear-j-104-88-1996.pdf.

had been repeatedly proven to be unsafe for women,[4] which automatically made it exponentially more unsafe for women of colour. I also spent time educating myself about the palpable racist undercurrent of the university, and took formal Black History classes to broaden my awareness and meet like-minded individuals of all hues.

By 2000, I was determined to not just suffer through the rest of my undergraduate experience, I was determined to thrive. I met and educated plenty of white peers who were unaware of their subtle (and not so subtle) racism. I'm not ashamed to admit that I shuffled and shucked my way through more than a few uncomfortable experiences to avoid unnecessary altercations. I was a low-key, 'social justice warrior' with little fear of exploring outside of the safe spaces for women and people of colour at the university.

During my re-education and transformation, I remember feeling like no one informed the entire population of Pennsylvania between Pittsburgh and Philadelphia that Jim Crow was over. The 'north' was not the bastion of open-minded liberalism that I was raised to believe it was.

Ella Es Una Negra Engreída (She's an Uppity Negro)
By the time 9/11 happened, I was a full-time, salaried Penn State University staff member and just a few credits short of my Bachelor's. None of that mattered, because the events of that day shattered me in ways I still see no path to recovery from. Less than six months later, a saintly friend of mine helped me pack my meagre belongings and move 'home.'

During my Pennsyltucky years, my parents retired to Florida, as it is where all New Yorkers (native or transplant) relocate to die. I could not move back home since NYC was still recovering in 2002, and the job market in tatters. Damaged

---

4   'At Penn State, one woman's rule at frat parties: Don't go upstairs', *Chicago Tribune*, 29 March 2015. www.chicagotribune.com/news/chi-penn-state-frat-parties-dont-go-upstairs-20150329-story.html.

and desperately needing my family, I swallowed my pride and moved back in with Mom and Dad in Orlando, Florida – the very same Florida that handed the 2000 election to George W. Bush and was rapidly amassing huge numbers of immigrants from Puerto Rico and Colombia.

Frantically attempting to get my life in order, I learned to drive at 25, finished my last undergraduate class and started my Master's coursework before the ink on my Bachelor's was dry. I applied for work and survived a myriad of torturous, entry-level positions. I got my Master's. I started to adult. All while Central Florida was becoming another hotbed of racial tension.

I was subjected to constant complaints from white neighbours and co-workers about how impossible it was to get help in Wal-Mart, because the staff was now predominantly Hispanic. I watched white flight from the more populous areas of Central Florida to high dollar areas of South Florida, or back up the coast to North Carolina and Virginia. Many of the high paying jobs also fled to Tampa, Miami, and other Florida cities with strong university presences to tap a more highly educated workforce. Florida has a reputation for being a state full of transients, but there were patterns that I failed to recognise to my detriment.

By 2005, the housing market was nearing its comical peak. Subprime mortgages bought many immigrants with poor English skills the American dream, and with that dream came a new pecking order. A shocking number of Hispanic friends and co-workers suddenly expressed conservative political views and were ready to vote Republican in the next election despite the party's moderate disinterest in the fastest growing population in America.

Meanwhile, the tide was turning in Florida. As a black woman, I've never even glanced the top of the pecking order, but I was brusquely reminded of my place while in a Colombian salon chair in Kissimmee. After I explained to my stylist how I wanted my hair treated, and corrected a few potential missteps, another stylist referred to me as 'Una Negra Engreída,' which my stylist found hysterical and vehemently agreed with. It was over a decade since I sat in a Spanish class, but it's not hard to figure out when you're being called a conceited black girl. I held my tongue, paid for my services, and got the hell out. Around a year later I got the hell out of Florida altogether.

Welcome to the Dirty

Working in a hostile environment at a Central Florida Real Estate company, I saw the mortgage industry collapse coming years ahead of time. Between the paltry job market in Florida and the impending financial bust, I decided to relocate to Raleigh, North Carolina. This area at the time was billed as the Silicon Valley of the South. Forbes may not realise that Raleigh and Durham are different cities in NC,[5] but they recognised that this area was the *Next Big Thing*.

This time around, my angelic father helped pack my meagre belongings, whilst Mom provided some financial and emotional support as I hurled myself from the nest (despite their protests) to start a new life in North Carolina.

North Carolina is just as much a part of the 'Dirty South' as Alabama, Louisiana, and Georgia. The difference *was* that once you got this close to the Mason Dixon, the racism *became* significantly more subtle. The sexism, however, was not nearly as bashful. But at this point, both are hanging out for all to see.

A perfect example of the difference between life up north and life down south is my experience in the different music scenes. In New York, Pennsylvania, and Florida, in part due to the size of the tours I went to see, I was never harassed. Even though crowds sometimes got aggressive, I was never singled out for any hate or physical aggression until I landed in the South.

---

5 'Raleigh, NC Area Honors and Accolades', *Live in Raleigh*. www. liveinraleigh.com/awards.php. Accessed 29 January 2017.

Starting in 2011, I made music photography a serious hobby. In 2014 I got the opportunity to cover larger, touring acts for a small, independent music site with a lean towards punk, metal, and hardcore. Now that I could cover larger, touring acts, I also got to mix with larger audiences. I was not shocked at the lack of diversity at metal and hardcore shows, but I was shocked at the brazen racism. The younger the average audience age skewed, the dirtier the stares, the more forceful the shoves, and the more intense the interrogation about why I was at the show in the first place. Complicate that with my sack of camera gear, the need to be close to the stage if there was no photo pit, and taking notes during a show, and I was a painted target for racists to take aim at.

The sexism I experienced at shows was far less aggressive than the racism, but many assume that a woman with a camera at a show is a groupie and couldn't possibly have a job to do. This applies not only to show attendees, but also to male photographers and videographers. Even within the (relative) safety of photo pits, I was pushed, jabbed, elbowed, and had 6 foot tall guys walk right in front of me as though I was invisible.

After two years of proximity to the music scene and its photography community, I saw racism and sexism here and within the music industry that I, naïvely, did not expect. Since music scenes can be a microcosm for their area, I experienced more than my fair share of racism and sexism outside of arenas and amphitheatres.

Between my arrival in NC in October of 2006 and former President Obama's election win in 2008, I experienced religious discrimination in the form of forced prayer at my place of employment in state government (because who gives a flying fig about the separation of church and state), multiple white male members of the management team in the same organisation taking credit for my work and comments about my skin colour and grade of hair from other women of colour at work (I am an uppity, high yellow negro after all).

I faced more inappropriate hair touching by white women in the workplace, and a white female co-worker flexing her privilege and crying for sympathy in a closed door meeting with our white male manager after she had a temper tantrum in the office with multiple witnesses. I was trapped in a dead-end state government job thanks to the mortgage industry collapse that flung America into a depression and was met with multiple, vicious 'nigger' laced tirades from men of all colours on various dating websites.

Between Obama's win in the 2008 election and his second win in the 2012 election, the pendulum swung again and I identified a consistently Republican-leaning North Carolina vote for Obama largely based on frustration about the number of North Carolinian soldiers lost in Afghanistan and Iraq and that a female Democrat took the Governor's mansion on a pro-education campaign. I was branded as an 'Angry Black Woman' in the workplace because I dared to stand up for myself, and had a note put in my state government 'file'.

There was a massive surge in my self-esteem and willingness to stand up for myself in the workplace. I got a new, rad, completely natural haircut and saw a surge in interest on dating websites from men who fetishised my skin colour and hair texture. I saw the birth of the Tea Party Movement, the bifurcation of the Republican party and the beginning of the whitelash as North Carolina voted for Romney and placed Pat McCrory in the Governor's mansion in 2012. Rednecks extinguished cigarettes on my Hybrid car's windshield wipers (because 'Murica!). The Tea Party and Birthers dragged the Republican Party far enough to the right to re-engage white supremacists and North Carolina's House Bill 2, otherwise known as Pat's Potty Police bill, came to be.

It was dizzying to watch America goose-step from hope to grope in less than four years.

Trump's Dirty South

As North Carolina's love affair with President Obama waned,

the Tea Party ran out of biscuits and fell out of favour with many of their constituents. The Republicans were fractured, had no clear leadership, stalled all attempts at Obama's progress, threw temper tantrums, and became a laughing stock. Is anyone *actually* shocked that a Cult of Personality like Donald J. Trump could rise to the forefront of this Republican Party caricature?

Trump inched closer and closer to the nomination in 2015, his racist and sexist rhetoric (let's face it, they go hand-in-hand) emboldened white supremacists. Rebranded as the so-called 'alt-right,' the nouveau white supremacists, especially those here in the South, carved a path straight to the presidency for The Donald.

The Dylann Roofs of the world are not born in vacuums, but are incubated by the David Dukes and Donald Trumps of the world.

Trump hypnotised the undereducated and fed the mentally malnourished rhetoric about helping the working class, about his prowess as a businessman, and a Nazi-esque slogan, 'Make America Great Again.'

As a black woman in the Dirty South, can someone please explain to me how America was great, when it was great, and when it stopped being great?

I make ~70% of the salary of white male counterparts in my industry and specialty. Statistics show that I am significantly less likely to be married in my lifetime than any white female. The establishment of whiteness as normal and the impact of slavery negatively affects black women disproportionately to every other ethnic group in almost every aspect of American life. I've spent my entire adult life seeking the Greatness of America, but I've yet to find it. Can I find this Greatness with Google Maps?

On November 9th 2016, I woke up to find that a man who mocked the disabled, threatened the freedom of the press, openly expressed blatantly racist and sexist sentiments, assaulted women, said women should be punished for having abortions, encouraged people at his rallies to perform Nazi salutes, asked

Russia to hack his opponent's campaign, and planned to ban Muslims from entering the country was now the President-elect.

America found out that not only were rust-belters and undereducated, rural southerners uninformed of the end of Jim Crow, but they sought to bring it back by electing Donald J. Trump. The most shocking fact, which many pundits are not addressing head on, is that Trump did not get elected solely by angry white men. Women are 52% of the population which means that:

- Women chose not to vote rather than voting to protect their rights
- Women voted for a man who is patently anti-woman
- Women voted for a white male saviour despite a mountain of evidence of sexism from the campaign and a long, documented history of the perils of giving men more power over them

Take a moment and ask yourself who are the real nasty women? Those of us who struggle to empower all women or those of us who empower men who ensure we remain second-class citizens?

When the Electoral College certified Trump's presidency on December 19th I lost my personhood, agency over my body, faith in our elections, and faith in women. Of that I lost, I am most devastated by seeing women enable someone like Trump. I haven't fooled myself either. Many of the women who voted for Trump still consider themselves feminists, but had an abject hatred of Hillary Clinton, and were willing participants in the whitelash resulting from Obama's presidency.

Situational feminism and the inability of white (surprisingly liberal) feminists to recognise their privilege, admit their fragility, and even see their unwillingness to address the issues of women of colour and women in the LGBTQ community are at the heart of the problems of marginalised women today. Every white woman who touched my hair without my permission, every attack in the photo pit, every targeted backpack search, they are products of the situational feminists who enabled Trump and have put America on this path. So, let me ask you again, who are the real nasty women?

FORAGING AND FEMINISM:
HEDGE-WITCHCRAFT IN THE 21ST CENTURY

Alice Tarbuck

I am in the kitchen, counting out rosehips. It is dark outside, and my partner and I keep forgetting ourselves with cross words. It is early December, but already the star in the window is shedding glitter onto the windowsill. On the kitchen work surface, a kilner jar is open, and I am counting out wizened red beads for tea. The rosehips (useful for 'all catarrhal, bronchial disorders') have been air-dried until leathery.[1] Against most advice, they haven't been shredded: the seeds and their infinite tiny hairs have not been sifted and separated. Keeping them whole is easier, and, if you're willing to steep them longer, they still release huge quantities of vitamin C. With honey and ginger, they're delicious and comforting.

These rosehips were never supposed to be picked. Three of us went out after dark, no torches, onto the cycle-path behind my friend's house. The lighting there is motion-sensitive, designed to aid cyclists and deter malingerers. In the six o'clock gloom of winter, the tarmac path stretched away in both directions, fading into black. There was a lot of giggling: nervousness and a feeling of transgression as the occasional cyclist zipped past. Picking by touch, we tore our hands up, probably dropped more onto the path than we did into Tupperware, eventually picked the remainder off by the light of a phone. Then we scurried home, drank wine by the fire, and felt brave and united.

Foraging is hardly a secret activity. In Scotland alone, there

---

1   Law, Donald. *The Concise Herbal Encyclopedia* (New York: St. Martin's, 1976), p. 81.

are a huge number of foraging courses, walks, group workshops. So popular has it become, that Scotland is now promoted as a destination for foraging: Visit Scotland invites the tourist to 'get your hands on these rich pickings of Scottish foraging' in order to participate in the foraging 'renaissance in restaurants and homes'.[2] *The Scotsman* newspaper published a guide to foraging in Scotland in 2015, complete with recipes.[3] Even Scottish National Heritage encourage foraging as a means of engaging with wild Scotland, writing that 'a growing interest in fresh, seasonal and local food is leading to a revival of wild-harvesting and foraging for ingredients for the table'.[4] This increase in popularity is so great that *The Guardian* reported it, in 2009, in terms of a gold rush: 'The Forestry Commission estimates that wild harvesting, including harvesting lichens and mosses for natural remedies and horticulture, is worth as much as £21m a year'.[5] This rapid growth comes, of course, with its own difficulties, and has led the Forestry Commission to 'promote wild foods with a code of good practice, to ensure the increasing number of foragers harvest carefully and, where needed, with the landowner's permission'.[6]

So foraging is back. Concerns about ethical food consumption, particularly in terms of global transportation and the working conditions of pickers, have spurred individuals to look locally

2   Clark, Sarah. 'Forage for your supper' *Visit Scotland*, 4 June 2015. www.visitscotland.com/blog/scotland/foraging/.

3   Edwards, Ian. 'Wild, Scottish and Free's Guide to Summer Foraging in Scotland', *The Scotsman*, 10 July 2015. foodanddrink.scotsman.com/food/wild-scottish-and-frees-guide-to-summer-foraging-in-scotland/.

4   'Foraging', Scottish Natural Heritage. www.snh.gov.uk/planning-and-development/economic-value/rural-enterprise/foraging/. Accessed 29 January 2017.

5   Carell, Severin. 'Wild harvest reaps big rewards in foraging rush' The Guardian, 27 April 2009. www.theguardian.com/environment/2009/apr/27/wild-food-foraging-reforesting-scotland.

6   Ibid.

for their food. This resurgence of interest is also a reaction to urban living, often without adequate green spaces or gardens. Feeling separated from nature, and from the processes of production, has led many people to look once more at what surrounds them. There is also an undeniable cachet to foraging: wild food has become a fashionable commodity. It can be, and indeed is bought, by restaurants at great price, albeit stripped of a certain authenticity. To have been outside, to have got your hands dirty, to own and use something that money can't buy: in a late-capitalist culture, that is prized indeed.

If gathering one's own wild food is not only popular and widespread, but also marketable, then why did we find it so thrilling? What on earth possessed us to do at night what perfectly rational people do on weekends, with rattan baskets and Barbour jackets? It didn't feel like foraging, at least not in the ways that Scottish National Heritage and *The Guardian* describe, which is not to say that we were doing anything particularly radical, or extraordinary, or that forgetting a torch earns you some sort of brownie points. But, disclaimers aside, what we did that night felt different. Trump was about to be elected. Britain had voted to leave the EU. Scotland was negotiating, once again, to have its voice heard. We were all scared – we are all still scared. We are young women, attempting to forge careers and lives and to think around big questions whilst the world swings rapidly to the right. Stealing out at night felt like an act of resistance, an act of seizing hold of the world and using it for ourselves. That we could go out, pick rosehips, which we knew the name, shape and qualities of, and then take them home, dry them and use them felt like an incredible gift. Really, it felt quite a lot like magic.

It feels quite a lot like magic that I can write this at all, in fact. Gathering herbs and plants for medicines, sharing them with friends, writing about it, all requires a huge amount of freedom, autonomy and education. After all, for a considerable period in Scotland's history, gathering herbs for medicine or magic, as a woman, could be a serious offence. On the 27th of January, 1591, not far outside Edinburgh, Agnes Sampson was tried as a witch, based on confessions extracted under torture. The list of accusations against her was staggering. Among them, that she 'healed by witchcraft Johnne Thomsoune in Dirletoun, though he remained a cripple' and that she 'cured Johnne Peiny in Preston by prayer and incantation'.[7] Most probably, she used herbs and plants gathered from the surrounding countryside.

Agnes Sampson was a midwife and local 'wise woman'. She offered counsel and natural medicine to those in her community who could not afford extortionate doctors fees. Such women (and indeed, men), whose presence had been part of village life for centuries, came under attack during the professionalisation of medicine in the sixteenth century. 'Wise women and their medicines', historian Andrew Wear writes, 'were often scoffed at by professionally trained doctors, nearly always male, who were anxious to protect their professional status'.[8] The skills of wise women and other local healers were minimised and dismissed, but their trade did not diminish. Many of their practices have since been debunked by contemporary medicine, such as widespread adherence to the 'doctrine of signatures', the belief that 'natural objects that looked like a part of the body could cure diseases that would arise there'. However, many of their cures were effective, as Wear notes, they included 'many naturally occurring ingredients that are medically useful'.[9] So, when dismissal of wise women failed to work, it was easier to vilify them.

It is not much of a step, after all, to suggest that healing skill is not healing at all, but witchcraft. Agnes Sampson would have

---

7   '27 January 1591 Trial of Agnes Sampson', Ryerson University. www.ryerson.ca/~meinhard/sampson.html. Accessed 29 January 2017.
8   Wear, A. *Knowledge and Practice in English Medicine, 1500 – 1800* (Cambridge: Cambridge University Press, 2000)
9   Ibid.

foraged, gathering what she needed from hedgerows to heal those who came to her. For this, she was forced to wear the Witch's Bridle, an iron headdress with four metal spikes that were inserted into her mouth so that speaking pierced her tongue and cheeks. She had all of her body hair shaved off by male interrogators in an attempt to find her 'witches' mark', and after several days of torture, confessed to being in league with the devil, and gave the names of others who were as well. She was, of course, only one of a huge number of women who were put to death during the witch trials of Scotland.[10]

The resurgence of foraging glosses over these historical connotations with witchcraft, precisely because foraging is now primarily associated with food. Access to free, reliable medicine has overturned the need for home remedies, and even these can be bought in 'alternative therapy' shops, dispensed by experts. Foraging, at least as portrayed in the mainstream media, is a middle-class leisure pursuit, rather than a matter of survival. And whilst it is fun to make wild garlic pesto, or to stew windfall apples, or to make elderflower cordial, it is impossible to pretend that these activities do not have historically gender and class-based implications.

There are, however, projects and individuals who are broadening perspectives on foraging, and respecting its nature as a historical practice. The Rhynie Woman collective, Debbi Beeson and Daisy Williamson, based in the North East of Scotland, and are engaged with promoting awareness of regional heritage through foraging practices. A recent project for Deveron Arts, 'Cooking the Landscape', saw them 'utilising foraging, honouring local food, traditional recipes and celebrations— to create a platform which promoted dialogue, skill sharing,

---

10 'The Survey of Scottish Witchcraft', The University of Edinburgh School of History, Classics and Archeology. www.shca.ed.ac.uk/Research/witches/introduction.html. Accessed 29 January 2017.

and the exchange of ideas'.[11] Rhynie Woman collective do not just forage: they engage with historic, local practices around gathering and preparation. By acknowledging the traditions that surround them, they are better able to understand foraging as a situated practice, and one that can enrich knowledge of local heritage. For the 'Cooking the Landscape' project, they took as a guiding quotation Michael Pollan's statement that 'the shared meal elevates eating from a mechanical process of fuelling the body to a ritual of family and community, from the mere animal biology to an act of culture'.[12] By re-introducing the idea of gathering, preparing and eating food as ritual practice, Rhynie Woman are able to explore and honour foraging traditions.

There is something mystical, magical about their foraging and cooking. They pose questions about wild foods and hospitality: 'What does it say of the host when served stinging nettles for tea; hidden inside a cream cake, their threat to sting ones tongue still present, lurking'.[13] Stinging nettles here are not being recognised for their culinary, or medicinal use, but rather for their symbolic potency. To eat a stinging nettle is to suffer pain, to be scolded for speaking out of turn, perhaps. It has the feeling of a punishment, or a curse – or even an echo of the Witch's Bridle. Of course, the true benignity of nettles – excellent for cleansing the blood – is here less important than their folkloric, symbolic impact. There is also the ripple of distrust that still spreads, even hundreds of years after Agnes Sampson's trial. 'What does it say of the host?' they ask: can we trust women who pick wild nettles not to hurt us, not to harbour and harness strange, wild power?

This strange, wild power might be frightening to those who eat the nettles, but it is important for those who gather them. I am aware, as I sort herbs or learn about mushrooms, or read a

---

11   Deveron-Projects, www.deveron-projects.com/rhynie-woman/. Accessed 29 January 2017.
12   Ibid.
13   Ibid.

friend's tarot, that perhaps what I am primarily interested in is power. Power against the constant, disempowering experience of being a woman. Power against catcallers, rapists, presidents who believe that sexual assault is acceptable. Power to see the future, or help a cold, or ease the winter blues, precisely because I have so little power in other areas. My tinctures will not break glass ceilings; my spells will not help women get the abortions they need, or equal pay, or anything else. But foraging in hedgerows and doing small magic with friends who I love feels empowering. It is like holding a secret in the warmth of your ribcage, and letting it glow right through you. And I am braver, I think, because of it. Because I am part of a community of strong women, finding ways to make ourselves powerful. I am braver in interviews, in meetings, in pitching for articles and negotiating boundaries. It is not in the least surprising that as the world seems to swing to the right, as the days seem to grow darker, that women are turning back to hedgerow magic, to attempting forms of community and ritual as part of working out how to fight back, how to remain empowered.

There are some places in Britain where hedge-magic and foraging for healing has never really gone away. In Cornwall, a strong tradition of Paganism and wise women persists. Cassandra Latham-Jones, for example, is the village wise woman of the Cornish village of St Buryan.[14] She offers a range of services, from creating charms with natural ingredients to counselling individuals who need help. Latham-Jones is a celebrant, tarot reader, and witch. In a filmed interview for the Open University's 'Religion Today' course, the camera follows Latham-Jones as she walks through the Cornish countryside, identifying plants to create a protection spell. Down-to-earth and entirely practical about her magic, Latham-Jones refers to

---

14   Latham-Jones, Cassandra. Grumpy Old Witchcraft, www.grumpy-oldwitchcraft.com/. Accessed 29 January 2017.

herself as a 'village witch', because it is the 'most relatable term', and says that she is asked about similar things that witches were asked about centuries ago: health, careers, romance.[15] Latham-Jones is dressed in black, and wears a black hat. She lives in a stone cottage, is married to a woman, and openly practices magic. In many ways, she is the epitome of Otherness, and yet she exists amid a community, serving their needs. Whether or not this community have an uneasy relationship with Latham-Jones is not discussed: the documentary and her website focus on the positive aspects of her practice. Latham-Jones does not conform to heteronormative ideals of femininity: she wears no makeup, wears masculine clothing and her magic does not relate to the domestic. She lives outside societal expectations, and is frank about the difficulty of making a living with her work.

Whilst she may not, therefore, be a traditional role model, she is nevertheless a very appealing figure. She is clearly passionate about her work, and feels empowered to live a life in accordance with her own desires and virtues, rather than those of society. Latham-Jones is an important figure in terms of the re-association of foraging with magic, and in terms of situating it historically. She is testament to the fact that foraging has been a traditionally female practice, associated with ritual and magic, not simple a leisure pursuit or interesting hobby.

By deliberately revitalising understanding of foraging as a radical, historically dangerous act, associated with arcane female knowledge and power, we can understand its potential as a feminist practice. Information about the landscape has, since the professionalisation of botany during the Victorian period, been primarily written and distributed by men. Male writers such as Tim Dee and Robert MacFarlane have spearheaded the current resurgence in nature writing over the past decade. Their

---

15   Woodland Wanderer, 'Open University Religion Today – Cassandra Latham Village Witch', YouTube, 21 April 2011. www.youtube.com/watch?v=h77DjKOZ3Z4.

approach to the natural world is that of the scientist or explorer: travelling through and documenting what is seen. Whilst bodily engagement with the landscape in these books is inevitable, there is no sense of engaging with the land in terms of what it produces. Picking berries, learning about the properties of different plants is secondary to the more scholarly concerns of the area's history and geography. Narrative immersion in landscape is engaging, and necessary in order to draw attention to our current environmental crisis, but the new nature writing can often be self-centred. A journey across mountains is, more often than not, related as a journey of self-discovery. This self-discovery is interesting and informative, but it obscures landscape as a site of plenty and bounty. Instead, it turns the focus back onto the male author and his adventuring.

Although she does not discuss foraging, Scottish nature writer Nan Shepherd, whose face was recently put onto the Scottish five pound note, radically refigures traditional nature writing tropes in her book *The Living Mountain*. Rather than walking through hills as an observer, Shepherd 'a localist of the best kind', seeks to communicate her 'acute perception' of the Cairngorm range.[16] Rather than walking 'up' the mountains, she walks instead 'into' them. Dissolving the ego, Shepherd seeks to be absorbed into the landscape, to understand it not through the accretion of knowledge but through direct haptic experience. She wishes to see, and become the mountain at the same time. Described by Macfarlane as a 'part-time mystic', interested in esoteric religions and Zen Buddhism, Shepherd has a quality of 'Otherness'. Not logical but emotional, not academic but perceptive, she is described in similar terms to wise women such as Latham-Jones. Rejecting an objective approach to her surroundings, she instead favoured immersion, intuitive under-standing and repeated visits. The mountains, for Shepherd, were

---

16   Macfarlane, Robert, 'Introduction', *The Living Mountain,* Nan Shepherd, (Edinburgh: Cannongate, 2011).

animate, and rather than learning about them, they taught her. This interest in walking, her enjoyment of isolation, the fact that she did not marry, all indicate an Otherness that seems to be held in common with other 'mystic' women. Any choice that removes them from the dominant cultural narratives and expectations placed upon them imbues these women with a sense that they are dangerous, somehow. They are the hostesses who might, perhaps, serve nettles.

So I stand in the shadow of all of these women. I do not face persecution like Agnes Martin; I do not have as much knowledge as Cassandra Latham-Jones. But I feel that any woman who decides to step outside what is demanded of her owes a debt to witches, to wise women, to women who walk alone in the hills. I am learning, from encyclopedias, from Tumblr, from friends and family. It does not matter if what I am doing is mostly nonsense, entirely nonsense, or not nonsense at all. What matters is that foraging connects me to the land and to friends, takes me outside, makes me look. Learning about the plants that grow around me, and how they might be used, lets me walk through my city with my eyes open. Preparing teas and drying herbs and burning red candles gives me a sense of power. Perhaps it is an illusion, or perhaps it is busy-work, or perhaps I really am doing magic.

The three of us felt so alive picking rosehips. Alive is how I want to feel, how rootling around in bushes or setting my intentions makes me feel. Feeling connected to the seasons, to the natural world, to the rhythms of growth and decay is helpful, grounding, reminds us that we are not alone on earth. There is beauty and bounty around us, if we look for it, and perhaps that is all the magic we need. Or perhaps, what we need is real magic, whether that comes in the form of resistance and community or the form of blackthorn charms and skullcap tinctures, and howling up at the moon.

FAT IN EVERY LANGUAGE

Jonatha Kottler

I am fat. That's probably the first thing you'd think when you see me. You might get past that after you get to know me.

One of my earliest memories is my grandmother, who would produce hundreds of homemade flour tortillas, and dozens of enchiladas swimming in cheesy, red chile sauce out of a kitchen the size of the walk-in closet of my last house in America. She used to call me *Juanita Gordita,* which means (because of the *-ita* diminutive in Spanish) 'Little Fat Jona.' I also remember my uncle telling me that only fat people had dimples (not true, by the way, but he was a Catholic priest and I was predisposed to consider his pronouncements as pretty authoritative). I tried to fill in the dimples of my cheeks with Play-Doh but it kept falling off. Actually, I was a pretty normal-sized kid. I didn't get really heavy until after my mother died, but I grew up thinking I was fat, and knowing it was a failure of character.

When you learn a foreign language you begin with the vocabulary of a child, able to describe the world and yourself in only the simplest of terms. When I learned French I was able to announce to the class, *'Je suis à courte'* (*I am short*); *'J'ai les cheveux brunettes'* (*I have brown hair*); *'Je suis americaine'* (*I am a female American*); *'Je suis grosse.'* Ugh. (*I am a fat lady*). And fat is a continuing condition, not like having a cold (*'j'ai un rhume'*) which will pass, but WHO I AM – a condition as unchangeable as where I was born or the colour of my eyes (*'mes yeux sont noisettes'*).

And French, I have to tell you, you're right. Fat is who I am: to people who haven't met me, ('the bathroom is over there, next to that fat lady') to people who know me, ('you looked *so good* when you lost that weight'); even to myself.

As an adult woman I have weighed between 140 pounds (10 stone – and you can bet that's the number that I put on my driver's licence) to 267 pounds (19.07 stone – outweighing the great Fat Icon Homer Simpson). At my lowest weight I was hired by Weight Watchers to ring up purchases and weigh women each week. On my name tag it said my name and the number of pounds I had lost: 'Jona – 112lbs.'

I was a 'Success Story™' for them and they wanted me to stand there as a beacon of hope to other women. It took me two years to lose that weight. At an average monthly cost of $41.00, plus food products (chalky-tasting caramel cookies were my favourite) and branded water bottles and special measuring cups – call it an easy $100.00/month which is $1200.00/year without counting grocery store microwave meals, cookbooks, sweatshirts, and drink stir-ins to make my eight glasses of water per day more festive.

The leader of my group used to call herself a 'three-time loser,' meaning she'd come to Weight Watchers three times before she kept the weight off. I would laugh along with everyone else (because this was my second time at Weight Watchers, which I'd chosen as a 'saner' approach than the Diet Center I'd gone to first – with its personal counsellor, daily weigh-ins, a strip of eight vitamin supplements per day and having to eat a Granny Smith apple before every meal that I ate). But being a 'three-time loser' isn't funny. It's their business model – a woman has some success at weight loss, and enjoys the support of other women at meetings. Then she 'slips up' and returns to her former weight, or maybe a bit more, gets disgusted with herself (she's 'gross' remember?) and goes back. Paying that $100, $500, $1,000 or $2,000 again and again.

And in the meantime she still feels fat. There's a lot of positive reassurance from society as she eats less and loses the weight. But there is very little support for maintaining the weight loss, and the praise for each pound she has lost dries up and she realises she is starving, working out 5-6 times a week and nothing replaces the satisfaction of the praise or the enjoyment of the eating. No wonder the weight gradually comes back. And it's even worse when something catastrophic happens, which it always does – it's life after all. For me the catastrophe was my father's death, estrangement in my family, and my best friend moving across the country. There was something inside me that was open and desperate, and I filled it up with some potato chips. And then thought I should probably go to a Weight Watchers meeting to put on the brakes. But the truth was, after two full years of weekly meetings, I knew everything they were going to say about portion control, and keeping a piece of fruit in my handbag, and always being prepared – as if somehow had I measured out my four ounces of brown rice in a better way my life wouldn't have fallen apart. I knew from experience, and also training as an employee (by the way, you get suspended if your weight creeps back) that no one there would or could or should help me with the emotional issues I was having. Food was only a salve.

So, fat again, I parted ways with Weight Watchers, which was hard for me. I'd had praise and success and measurement of my worth as my value to society rose with every pound I lost. And when Oprah bought a bunch of stock in it in October of 2015, I actually thought 'I should go back.' If it was good enough for Oprah – whose public struggles with weight have been a part of my own narrative my entire life – sign me up! It took a lot for me to hold back from signing up. I downloaded the app to my phone, and then deleted it.

One last Weight Watchers story. In my first try I had a group leader who lost fifteen pounds in 1971 when the diet included eating liver a minimum of once a week and eating up to four eggs per week but only before noon. (See the *Mad Men* season with 'Fat Betty' for additional hijinx). This leader told the same story every week – about a snow crash in Canada where a plane went down and of the eight people on board seven died. The fat woman on the plane had lived off of her 'fat pantry' (the leader's phrase) until she was rescued. This leader thought she was telling me that I was walking around in a non-emergency life with emergency rations in my pants. But really, every week, I used to think, 'Ha! The fat girl survives!'

Being fat in America means you are a problem to be solved and a rich market to reap. Corporations, who make everything from supplements to weights to diet foods to clothing to the fake 'Enorme' perfume for plus-size women that Tina Fey satirised in her television show *30 Rock*, fill women with hate and self-loathing so they can make more and more money off of them losing and gaining the same pounds over.

When I moved to Holland I had gained weight from my days of being a before and after photo shoot for a magazine (reader, I was!) but didn't weigh as much as at my top weight. In Amsterdam, everything about me was out of place. My attempts at practicing my Dutch were met with scorn and an immediate switch to English. Even my raincoat – a bright yellow – blared out my presence against the sea of black coats and grey sky.

But nothing made me stand out more than my size. Every sidewalk, tram car, and restaurant chair made it clear that in the land of the very tall and very slim I was a sphere, like Violet Beauregarde in yellow, rolling around and taking up more than my share of space. Which is not '*doe normaal*' (Dutch for 'just be normal, do like everyone else').

Worse yet, struggling and homesick, I was, to the people who saw me, living proof of their worst American stereotypes. Suddenly I wasn't just *me*, an overweight woman who was singled out as fat in her own country, but the manifestation of the fat, lazy, loud, insincere, stupid Americans that they always knew existed.

One day, about twelve weeks after blowing up my whole life and moving my family to what seemed like a very hostile environment, my son and I decided we would go to the cinema and see *The Great Gatsby* to cheer ourselves up and feel less homesick. We did what we sometimes did at home – skipped dinner to have popcorn for dinner instead. Already flummoxed by having to pre-order our tickets for assigned seats on a Dutch website (none of these were cinema-hurdles back home where you'd just walk up and buy a ticket) we arrived at the cinema. We bought the largest popcorn (which is in fact a product they sold – we didn't bring our own trash barrel and ask to have it filled) and settled in to enjoy our treat. I felt a tap on my shoulder, which was strange since I knew a total of three people in the entire country. I spun around, startled, and the Dutch man sitting behind me said, 'Are you going to eat all of that? I see why you are so fat.'

I hadn't spoken to him, bumped against him, or ever seen him before in my life. His words left me shaking, unable to enjoy the film, unable to touch the food. Why did he feel the need to say that to me? The Dutch frankness they are so well-known for often touched me in this way. People telling me that I was ordering too much food at the grocery store, or if there was a final piece of food on a communal plate saying, 'You will be the one to eat that, I suppose.'

Here's a fact: fat people know they are fat. We live it every single moment of every day. Whether it has a physical cause like a prescription drug that saves your life, but makes you gain weight; or an emotional or psychological one; or is even simply a deliberate choice, we know we are fat. And if we ever forget it for a moment, there is a whole world to remind us. And you can say it aside, or in your own language '*dikke vrouw*' (big fat lady), or just think it while looking at us in disgust, but we always know that you know it, too.

I've been in Scotland for two years, where people are generally a little heavier (and they get plenty of knocks for it in the media, especially the English media, who like to poke fun at which vegetables people eat or don't eat, and who reduce Scottish cuisine to a deep-fried Mars bar. But really the people here are individuals: tall and short and thin and fat and foreign and local and... individual). On our first bus ride, the photo of the family advertising using the bus for an outing featured a heavier-set man. My husband leaned over to me and said, 'Hey, look, we are allowed here!'

Scotland is a chilly place, but people here will always make a cup of tea for you and will never fail to offer you a slice of cake to go with it. Cake, in fact, is part of the national pastime. Lovely, jammy cake; or lavender and lemon; or sticky chocolatey cake, all meant to be picked up with your hands. (My son always says of Scotland, 'They eat pizza like cake and cake like pizza.') It's hard to navigate hospitality versus healthfulness. And I felt that I really needed to learn to make a good Victoria Sponge to fit in. Which involves eating more than a few sub-par ones.

I wanted to get off on a good foot with our new landlords when we moved here (of course we didn't, really. Pro tip: never live in the flat below your posh landlords – it will confirm for them, physically, that you are beneath them). When I was making a trip home to the States, I bought a special toy one of the children wanted – a yellow New York taxicab. I delivered it to them with friendly American charm and as I walked away I heard the child say, to her not-model-thin mother, 'Why is our new neighbour such a fat lady?' Her mother said, 'She is a fat lady, but don't say it.'

So, today I'm fat. And American. And in Scotland. One or more of those things might change (like my address: moving away from awful landlords, and too-frank Dutchmen, and the undue influence of Oprah). But what really has to change is how many fucks I give about all of this. Here are more fun facts: I have friends. I am loved by an excellent partner (who also finds me sexy). I have a terrific kid. My cats like that I am cosy to sit on. I cannot define my own value by the amount of space I take up at a given moment. I cannot speak to myself in that language anymore.

AFTERBIRTH

Chitra Ramaswamy

When I was nine months pregnant, something unexpected happened to my expecting self. My midwife was in the midst of giving me a membrane sweep... Hold on a minute, a *what*, some of you will ask? One of the many peculiarities of pregnancy – which lest we forget is the precursor to all our existences – is that the language does not cross the border into the non-pregnant world. The one in which everyone who is 'of woman born', to quote Shakespeare's Macbeth, lives. Such mysterious words as *Braxton Hicks, colostrum, effacement, lochia, mucus plug*, or *vernix* remain as contained in the curiously silenced hinterland of pregnancy and birth as the foetus is within the womb. There is no language in that dark liquid place, and it turns out that beyond the uterine wall we pregnant women tend not to spill our secrets either. Even when our waters break, the silence remains intact. This is why being pregnant is an education in language as much as a tutorial on the body. I only know what a mucus plug is because I have formed and expelled one.

So. A membrane sweep. Often referred to as a 'natural' procedure (there is a lot of bandying about of that notoriously tricky word in pregnancy), a membrane sweep is offered to women who are overdue in the hope of inducing labour. A midwife inserts two fingers into the vagina and sweeps them around the cervix, releasing prostaglandins that may kickstart labour. The sweep can only be performed if the cervix is already beginning to dilate, thin and shorten; this is the mysterious 'effacement' I just mentioned. Does it hurt? Only in the way a cervical smear does: momentarily, a minor but deeply personal affront.

Afterbirth

There I was at the height of an unusually hot summer in Edinburgh having the first of what would be three sweeps. I was around ten days past my due date, perfectly healthy, frantic, broiled, and enormous. I was determined to get this baby out, a tenacity like no other I've experienced in my life that would endure all the way through my labour to the birth of my son. Quite a few days later.

Anyway, I lay on my back in my local NHS community centre in Leith, my belly rearing up ahead of me in a majestic and rather brutal reminder of the ascent to come. A sledgehammer of a metaphor, like so many in pregnancy. My midwife, after a certain amount of digging around, pronounced my cervix a centimetre dilated. Victory in a measurement the length of my thumbnail. Only another nine centimetres to go until I could push the baby out. I was disproportionately ecstatic. Early labour was happening, even if I could not feel it.

Then came the unexpected.

'I can feel your baby's head,' she told me.

'Erm, what?'

'I'm feeling it right now,' she continued, and a lovely smile appeared on her face, and soon enough, transferred to mine. I laughed in excitement, shock, and perhaps a little horror. The baby was inside me, had been felt by no one but myself, yet was suddenly, and without warning, being touched by someone else. Someone from the outside world. This one. The one in which everyone 'of woman born' lives. It had never occurred to me that you could feel a baby while it's still inside the womb. Now this most obvious of facts, the point of the whole bloody nine months – that there was a baby right there, between my legs, on the precipice of coming out, of beginning a life separate but indelibly connected to mine – struck me as extraordinary. It blew me away. It still does, when I think of it.

'What's he like?' I asked dumbly, as though the baby – *this baby* – was a man she had just met in a bar.

'His head feels lovely and smooth,' was her intriguing reply.

Chitra Ramaswamy

* * *

I recount this story in the final chapter of my book, *Expecting*, a memoir of nine chapters for the nine months of pregnancy. It's a strange book, part travelogue of pregnancy, part investigation of art, literature and family, part nature writing about the bodyscape, part search for metaphor and identity, part thriller. This seems appropriate for an experience so strange yet so, well, self-evident, we've forgotten to revel in its curiosities. Or rather, we've been told not to. Pregnancy is shrouded in shame, fear, misrepresentation, metaphor, dogma and lies. The message covertly transmitted to women is that to write about it is to be self-indulgent, conventional, narrow-minded, gross, unintellectual, and boring. To be a nasty woman. To revel in the fecundity of one's ovaries: how embarrassing. How yucky. Pregnancy is not unlike death in the way it is treated, or rather mistreated, in society. Which makes sense when you think about it. Birth and death: the first and last chapters that are the most difficult to write. 'Birth, life, and death,' wrote the African-American novelist Toni Morrison, 'each took place on the hidden side of a leaf.' Except something occurred to me while I was writing *Expecting*: while death happens to all of us, birth happens to women. The stigma multiplies like the cells of a fertilised egg in the petri dish of misogyny.

Throughout my pregnancy this lack of understanding about what exactly the business of growing, sustaining, and birthing a life actually entailed manifested as shock, awe, bewilderment and fear. Time and time again, I found myself thinking *I can't believe I never knew this*. That, in no particular order, my hair would stop falling out, I had a tilted uterus, my breasts would leak thin watery milk months before the baby was born, and that you can *see* as well as feel a contraction. Even at the arse end of my final month, lying on a bed having a membrane sweep, my pregnant body had the capacity to blow me away.

And since writing *Expecting* and encountering women, some who are currently pregnant, some whose pregnancies took place decades ago, and some who have never been pregnant (and also, by the way, lots of men), I've realised how much the experience of not-knowing is shared. The silence is handed down through generations. We are literally instructed to forget the pain of childbirth once the baby is here. And so we all seem to walk around in a stupefied state, hermetically sealed in our nine-month stories as the babes are in our wombs. Meanwhile society seeks to tell us who we are, what we should be doing, eating, saying, thinking, feeling and how we should be birthing. How to be natural. It is an overwhelming combination: so much going on inside, so much coming at us from the outside. The result? Ever more silence.

I began to realise why pregnancy is such a richly metaphorical state, heavy with meaning and euphemism as well as with child. By the late 14th century to be pregnant also signified being convincing or weighty. Consider, for example, the pregnant pause. Consider all the ways of talking about pregnancy, across cultures and generations, without using the actual word: *enceinte, in pig, up the duff, bun in the oven, knocked up, up the pole* (which was first used in James Joyce's Ulysses). In the first line of her 1959 poem 'Metaphors', written while pregnant with her first child, the poet Sylvia Plath wrote of being 'a riddle in nine syllables'. Metaphors can be wonderful, but they can also be absurd, reductive, and they can obscure the truth.

In writing a book about pregnancy and birth I wanted to seek out the existing metaphors in art, literature, film and culture, come up with some of my own, and maybe even abandon them altogether and tell a different, more sideways story. One book that hugely influenced me had absolutely nothing to do with pregnancy and birth. *The Living Mountain*, written by an Aberdonian teacher called Nan Shepherd in the last years of the Second World War. A deeply sensual book about the Cairngorm massif and one woman's lifelong acquaintance with its minutiae:

its alpine flowers and tight little balls of pine needles formed by a river's currents, nooks, crannies, corries, the weather, light, and abundance of water swelling from the hills that 'does nothing, absolutely nothing, but be itself'. It seemed to me that this was the way to write about pregnancy: to reflect on the mystery of the inside of the belly-mountain, to meander through the nine months as Shepherd writes of having gone round the plateau 'like a dog in circles to see if it is a good place.' And so she concludes: 'I think it is, and I am to stay up here for a while.'

There is a name for this kind of writing: sensual, aimless, feminist to its tough and embodied core. Writing that attempts to bridge the gap between women's experience and language's inability to describe it. In the 70s the French theorist and feminist Helene Cixous called it 'ecriture feminine' and urged women to write in the 'white ink' of their milk… 'not about destiny, but about the adventure of such and such a drive, about trips, crossings, trudges [and] abrupt and gradual awakenings…'[1] To treat pregnancy and birth, which historically have been denigrated, neglected, and shrouded in shame, as subjects worthy of philosophical inquiry as death, nature, war or any other weighty (dare I say pregnant) experience, is to attempt a kind of ecriture feminine. *Expecting*, I hoped, would be nature writing in the spirit of Nan Shepherd, in which the gravid body would stand in for the landscape, the living belly for the living mountain. And it would not only be for pregnant women, mothers, or even women but rather an everyperson story of how we all began.

It would also be a social document. My pregnancy, like my life, is a product of my time. A pregnancy experienced by a bisexual Indian woman from London, living in Scotland, civilly partnered to a white Scottish woman, with a resulting child who is mixed race and has two mothers. It's a story of difference,

1   Warhol-Down, Robyn, Herndl, Diane Price. *Feminism Redux: An Anthology of Literary Theory and Criticism* (Rutgers University Press, 2009), p. 424.

I suppose, but the point is that the nine chapters are the same.

Nevertheless the difference exists and it should be named, marked, and celebrated for it is enshrined in rights that are hard-won and as fragile as a newly fertilised egg. Mine is a pregnancy and birth happening here and now, in the United Kingdom, in the tumultuous second decade of the 21st century. So different to a pregnancy taking place in a developing country, where 99 per cent of all maternal deaths occur and where approximately 830 women die every single day from preventable causes related to pregnancy and childbirth. Or in a previous century before the advent of pain relief, when labour pains were viewed as a punishment from God or when puerperal or childbed fever – spread by physicians' unwashed hands – claimed the lives of so many women, including Mary Wollstonecraft, who died days after giving birth to her daughter, Mary Shelley, following a doctor's removal of part of her placenta. Or in a future when the reproductive and maternity rights I have known in my lifetime are threatened, denied, perhaps even eradicated by a handful of emboldened white men.

For suddenly that future, which for women is always lurking on the horizon like a mist-laden threat, draws dangerously close. Watching the President of the United States reinstate the Global Gag Rule on his first official working day, it felt as though it might be here. The rule bans international NGOs[2] from providing abortion services or offering information about abortions if they receive US funding. And US funding matters: America is the single largest donor to global health efforts. So this hateful rollback of women's rights, by a man who once said women should be punished for abortion,[3] will put thousands

2   Non-Governmental Organisation
3   Kertscher, Tom. 'In Context: Transcript of Donald Trump on punishing women for abortion', *Politifact*, 30 March 2016. www.politifact.com/wisconsin/article/2016/mar/30/context-transcript-donald-trump-punishing-women-ab/.

of doctors, midwives, and nurses all over the world in the unthinkable position of having to choose between offering family planning care that includes abortion and losing critical funding. It is no exaggeration to say that women will die as a result: unsafe abortions kill tens of thousands of women every single year.[4]

One response to the image of the President signing the executive order noted that 'As long as you live you'll never see a photograph of 7 women signing legislation about what men can do with their reproductive organs.'[5] Well, quite: do we need any greater evidence of the ancient and inescapable workings of the patriarchy than this single chilling photo? It represents a war on women: on their choices, lives, and on their very internal organs. It is hard to think of a more unassailable right than the possession of one's own body. Of one's own womb. And as wombs are the source of all life, this is a war on humankind too. On all of us. Let's not forget the appalling fact that the hands that signed that executive order are the same ones that grabbed pussy.

What can we do in response but march, resist, hope, care, and – if we are so inclined – write? Write who we are, what our bodies can and cannot do, and what we want to do with them, without shame or apology. 'If we have the habit of freedom and the courage to write exactly what we think,' wrote Virginia Woolf, 'then the opportunity will come.'

Still, it is not easy. I foolishly thought *Expecting* would be – to use a pregnancy word – *viable* as a story because it is universal, it happens to a lot of women, all of us, male and female, began life

4 'Preventing unsafe abortion', *WHO*. www.who.int/reproductive-health/topics/unsafe_abortion/magnitude/en/. Accessed 04 February 2017.

5 Cosslett, Rhiannon Lucy. 'This photo sums up Trump's assault on women's rights', *The Guardian*, 24 January 2017. https://www.theguardian.com/commentisfree/2017/jan/24/photo-trump-womens-rights-protest-reproductive-abortion-developing-contries [sic].

in the womb, and it had not been done before. Since writing the book, however, the stigma surrounding this subject has reared its head – you might say crowned – over and over again. I've been told, sometimes explicitly, that this fundamental experience is too niche, too risky, too bog-standard, that women are only interested in their pregnancies until the baby comes along, that motherhood eclipses everything, that pregnancy can never be more than a prologue, that there is no market for this sort of thing, and so on. How can this be true? How can birth be less valuable, interesting, rich, or complex than the life that proceeds it? Than the death that ends it?

Leo Tolstoy – a man 'of woman born', no less! – nailed it when he wrote in *Anna Karenina*, which incidentally contains one of the most vivid and long childbirth scenes in literature, that the joy and grief of witnessing birth and death 'were like holes in this ordinary life, through which something higher showed.' A 'hole in this ordinary life' is perhaps the best description of pregnancy and birth I have come across, and what is writing for but to dive in to the hole, burrow, and excavate. To go around, as Nan Shepherd wrote of her beloved Cairngorms, 'like a dog in circles' to see if it – the mountain, the hole, the pregnancy, or any experience we deem significant – is a good place. And if it is, why not do as Shepherd does and stay a while.

Expecting: The Inner Life of Pregnancy is published by Saraband.

HARD DUMPLINGS FOR VISITORS

Christina Neuwirth

My maternal line has come down to my sister and I. Mama died when she was 54. She had breast cancer. This was four years ago, on New Year's Eve, 2012. Oma died in January of 2016. She was 94. A permanent change is a strange thing. It's difficult to wrap my head around the fact that, for the rest of my life, they will be gone.

I don't know what I want to tell you in this essay. In some way it's important to me to tell you all about them, so you know them. That's the thing I felt most keenly when they passed away: I want their memory to live on. Before my grandmother died, I thought her death would propel me into pregnancy almost immediately: *I need to continue our line. Once my maternal grandmother and mother are gone, it's up to me, as my mother's oldest daughter.* That didn't happen. I have focused my energy differently. For one, I have been cooking more Austrian food than ever.

When I first moved to Scotland I was excited about all the different food that was suddenly available. I made stir fries and curries for almost every meal. Don't get me started about the wonders of being able to order macaroni cheese and have it served with chips on the side, and sometimes even a slice of garlic bread!

But recently I've made more of the food I grew up with. Strudel, with blitzed slices of toast for the breadcrumbs. Ćevapčići, which is mince rolled into sausage-like shapes (although mine looked more like eggs), served with mashed potatoes with a sauce made from ketchup, pickles and mustard, salad on the side dressed with pumpkin seed oil, dark green and fragrant. Three types of Christmas cookies (my auntie B makes ten). Bell peppers stuffed with rice, onions, caraway seeds and smoked paprika, boiled in tangy, runny tomato sauce. And soups! Frittatensuppe, a clear broth with thin strips of crêpes.

And Grießnockerlsuppe. The holy grail of soup, a clear broth in which you cook dumplings made from semolina, egg and bits of parsley or chives. The dumpling mixture needs to be an exact consistency: too runny and it'll dissolve, making a cloudy soup with a floating softness of semolina. Too thick and it'll make for tough dumplings. The kind that, when you try and break into them with the edge of your spoon, go flying across the table-cloth leaving a broth-y trail of splashes. My mum's Grießnockerl always turned out perfectly – huge, fluffy quenelles of eggy semolina-y loveliness. She'd grind the semolina herself, with her miniature grain mill set to coarse.

Every dumpling was perfect for us, her family, but whenever a visitor would come over, the dumplings would be hard. Maybe it was because she would rush the mixture and wouldn't let it sit long enough for the semolina to soak up the egg – or maybe it's just the effect of rushing to perform, to impress her friends. In either case, I've inherited that trait. When I made Grießnockerlsuppe for my friends this year, the dumplings were tough. Friends, if you're reading this: it's because I was trying too hard. It's because I've inherited that from my mother.

The infuriating lack of precise recipes is something I've inherited from my grandmother. Many of Oma's recipes existed only in her head. I don't know if anyone else kept old cake in the freezer so they could grate it into the breadcrumbs of a strudel. She'd dictate a recipe to me on the phone and say, 'If you have an egg, use an egg. If you don't have an egg, just make it without.' She had a lot of recipes written down, but the real way to learn them was to make something with her. Not long before she died we made strudel together – she delegated, I stirred, combined, cut, sprinkled. She couldn't say how much flour to use for the pastry, so instead she poked it and said,

'Look, it needs to spring back like this for it to be right'.

She had a wood-burning stove in her kitchen, above which sat eight big ceramic drawers set in a wooden cabinet. They were white with a blue trim, and labelled Zucker, Kaffee, Mehl, and so on. The Kaffee one was where she kept the cash that she'd slip us when our parents weren't looking. She also had an electric stove and oven. There was a woven basket with kindling and newspaper near her bench. Her vegetable knife, the small one, had a flat plastic handle from the time she left it sitting on her stove and it melted.

In 2015, before Christmas and about a month before she passed away, she wanted to give me some money. She said she'd hidden it under the cupboard so her son and her carer wouldn't find it. She had stuffed some cash into a little zip bag and tossed it in the gap between the cupboard and the floor. Fetching it with the skiing stick she used to help her walk, I found the pouch was empty. She'd forgotten that her son was looking after that money, too, just like he was taking care of all her bills. It was for the better. He was helping, I knew that. I couldn't help but sympathise with her, feeling helpless and confused.

Both Oma and Mama were strong women, kind-hearted and aggressively hospitable. They were the glue that kept me fused to my immediate and wider family while always travelling, always longing to be somewhere else. I used to rush home to say 'Hi' to Mum and after her death, I began rushing home to Oma instead. Upon receiving good news, I'd phone my dad, my sister, and her. Oma would often tell me what she felt my mum would think about what I was up to, which was a comfort and a gift. I told my counsellor that if she died too, there would be an extra burden on me.

I have a little sister, and there are a lot of other women in my extended family. But somehow, speaking to my counsellor after my mum's death, I felt that if my Oma died I would crumble to pieces. Losing Mama when I was 22 left my emotions free-falling and moral compass confused. I lost direction and didn't have her to turn to when I needed guidance. I didn't get to tell her I had been accepted into a creative writing master's. Six months after her death, when I moved from Austria to Scotland, I didn't get to ask her for advice on packing, or phone her when I was homesick.

In many ways I think my Mama would be glad I am here in Edinburgh. She was very supportive of my writing, and often talked about wanting to write a book herself. She travelled quite a bit when she was younger, as part of a folk dancing and singing group. I imagine them all crammed into a tiny bus (in my mind's eye it's a beige Volkswagen van) singing and tapping stockinged feet on the way to Estonia, Denmark, France, Spain, Wales. I've been living away from Austria for more than three years now, but often worry I've betrayed the memory of these two women I come from. They tried so hard to make a home in the village I left. My grandmother lived there for nearly 94 years. We used to play near the house where she grew up. My mum was born in the house next door to where we built ours. The layers of history in the village are palpable, and every time I explain the layer upon layer I get choked up with memories of how thick the air feels, how heavy, how knitted into every house and tree. The walnut tree next to the driveway leading to our house (salmon pink, my mum picked the colour) was the tree she sat in when she studied for her A-levels.

Here's what I've learned from my mother: give in and you'll be the smarter person at the end of the argument. If you don't give in that makes you stubborn. Be bigger. Compromise. Give in. As I move through the world of work, creative and otherwise, I've realised I don't want that. It makes me feel guilty. I have also come to suspect that my mum didn't live by this either. I remember her crusade to get the heating fixed in a school she taught in: the boiler was sending toxic fumes into her classroom, causing headaches in a lot of her pupils and triggering migraines in herself most days. She argued even when many people on the school board thought she was imagining it. She got her way. She didn't give in. It was the right thing to do.

My grandmother was always old to me. When I was born she was 69, which seemed old at the time. My mum often told me to go ask Oma about the war, but I never did. The time I did, I asked about the most famous story, the one that became family folklore. How my Oma escaped the Russian allies on a horse. It turns out she wasn't on horseback, but in a little horse-drawn cart, with a woman who was going back to what would become the Czech Republic. They ran because the Red Army was notorious for raping women. At the Czech border, my Oma left the cart, found a bicycle, and kept going. She slept in sheds and barns and wherever she could find a roof over her head. One night, she left the bicycle leaning against the barn door and the next day it wasn't there. So she walked. She walked across the country until she arrived at an area controlled by the British. Then she boarded a train and went straight home.

In 1945, she was 24.

That's younger than I am now.

I looked up the Red Army rapes on Wikipedia recently and the figures are absolutely sickening. I am so glad my Oma escaped, but I am hurting for all the women who didn't. I cannot imagine what it must have felt like for her to fear that if she couldn't run away this might have been her fate.

I'm living in Scotland, which didn't vote for Brexit, but I'm also living in the UK, which did. I'm from a country that very nearly elected a right-wing proto-fascist president, but then, by a hair's breadth, didn't. I often think about how brave it was for my grandmother to be the kind of person she was. She opened her house to foreigners back in the fifties, sixties, seventies, in a tiny village in rural Austria. I think of how my mother, when she was 18, nearly married a man from Iran and nearly moved to Tehran, but then ended up not going because she was homesick – and my grandmother was on her side. I think about how my mother also nearly married a man from the south of France. I think about how the open borders I grew up with – the same ones we might lose in my lifetime – are an achievement of her generation. She grew up with the iron curtain.

I've left that small village behind, for now. It's a sanctuary whenever I visit. I'm lucky to have my childhood home intact, waiting for me to come home. There's a small pain in my side when I remember how hard my grandmother and mother worked to make their home in that village. How my mother suffered in those nine years that we didn't live there, when she was newly married to my dad, living in a different village a ten-minute drive up the hill from ours, always feeling like she wanted to live right next to her mother. I fear that it says something about me that I chose not to live there, or near there, or even in the same country, for now. Both Oma and Mama were Catholic while I'm agnostic, most days. I feel a pang of guilt when I go to church at Christmas and don't mean the words I'm singing. It doesn't stop me from lighting a candle, or kneeling and standing up when these are required.

Death is forever. Many of the conditions, experiences and events that affect my life in this century are fleeting. Some of the conditions that I'm affected by are changeable, or I hope they are, anyway. But this absence, more than anything else, is permanent.

It is weird to identify permanence when I worked hard to that change is inevitable, an opportunity, and that it's okay. Before my mother died I'd already lived in Austria, New Zealand, and Denmark. I was used to leaving people behind.

Nothing lasts forever.

Except this.

I will never again have a mother or a grandmother.

They have died and for the rest of my life they will be dead.

When I met my partner I thought, *wow, this is it, this is forever,* but a little voice at the back of my mind stopped me before I tricked myself into believing that that love could last for the rest of my life. I'd like it to, but I just don't know. Things change. Except this: these two people aren't coming back.

When I wrote my first story at university I translated it for Oma. It had a swear in it. I left it in – it was only a small one – and she commented on it, saying that the story would be better without the swear. I hope my swearing doesn't disappoint them. I hope I can make them proud, looking beyond the unfairness and unbelievableness of me being alive when they aren't. When I bake a cake from an old recipe I bake it for them. And when I have an egg, I use it.

RESISTING BY EXISTING:
CARVING OUT ACCESSIBLE SPACES

Belle Owen

Although I was born with a disability, it wasn't till the tenth year of my life that I became a wheelchair user. Pseudoachondroplasia (a genetic disorder that effects bone growth) made me significantly shorter than my peers, it weakened my ligaments, bowed my bones, filled my joints and my back with pain that seemed to worsen as I grew older. When I started falling behind on class trips and family outings and had reached the age where sitting in a stroller was no longer feasible for the independent person I was trying to become, my parents started the process to get me a wheelchair.

I remember trying first a manual, then a power wheelchair. A power wheelchair was the obvious choice, thanks to my short arms and lax joints. I felt taller, because I was. I felt faster, because I was. I felt less fragile, less likely to be trodden on, pushed around or ignored. I felt free – for a moment.

No one in my family had a disability, similar to mine or otherwise. I was enrolled in a public school with a diverse group of students, but none that seemed to need all of the accommodations I did.

Still too young to fully grasp the opinions behind the attitudes and remarks from adults that weren't always kept out of my earshot, I later came to understand that some family and teachers rejected the decision and the change in my life. They didn't recognise my wheelchair to be the tool of liberation that I did.

At that time, my parents had signed our family up to be members of the Little People's Association of Australia (now known as the Short Statured People's Association) so that we could interact and learn from families in the same position as ours. A large majority of the members had a different condition to me. Not only were they on average, slightly taller, they didn't seem to experience many of the issues I had. At our next function, the weight of being the only wheelchair user in the group felt heavy on my shoulders. The people who I considered my closest peers and the most likely to understand, didn't see liberation either – they saw defeat.

I'm often asked if I experienced bullying when I was younger, because of my disability. Surprisingly, none of it came from kids. I always had a sort of innate knowledge that as someone who was going to be physically small I would have to be assertive and make my voice symbolically loud to be truly heard. As a kid I was outgoing, friendly and, to a certain extent, popular.

While a completely able-bodied group of friends throughout primary and high school were supportive and allowed me a fairly 'regular' teenage experience, it also deeply ingrained in me the societal expectation of striving for normality. The assumption is that normality is what's right, what's desirable, and what belongs – everything most teenagers want to emulate. When people told me they didn't even notice my wheelchair, when they announced that they 'didn't even see' my disability, I took it as the compliment that they intended. At the time, it felt like success.

This entrenched quest for normality, however problematic later in life, also gifted me an inextinguishable determination that I should never be excluded or miss out on what my peers experienced, including the quintessential teenage experiences of sex, drugs and especially rock and roll. When friends started bands, my parents would be the one to drive us all to the shows because they were the ones with the wheelchair accessible van. When the shows were booked at upstairs venues or underground clubs, friends carried me upstairs and I sat on amps away from mosh pits. However, if I was able to get my wheelchair into the gigs, I crushed myself into the crowd with everyone else, wearing the post-mosh bruises like a badge of honour. I never took no as an answer, from myself or from anyone else.

With my growing independence, I began to experience the world outside of my high school/local punk and hardcore band bubble and came to understand that while it was expected that I should want to be 'normal', it was something I very obviously wasn't. I started having to graciously accept unnecessary help. Frequently people would interfere with actions I was, and am, perfectly capable of, like taking my purse from my hands while I was in the middle of paying for a meal, a coffee, whatever. They'd finish the transaction for me, hand over my money to a cashier and when I would be taken aback by a stranger pulling my money from my hands, people would turn, call me ungrateful, tell me it was the last time they would help 'the disabled'. I began to feel the burden and responsibility of being a representative of everyone in a similar situation.

When out alone, I fielded questions from strangers. 'What happened?' 'Why are you like that?' It made me uncomfortable, but rather than sour the general public on every wheelchair user, I'd fumble my way through a feeble explanation.

The shows I went to got bigger. With larger, international bands came larger, unfamiliar venues and a quick lesson that there was no place for me there. No longer in small clubs with friends both playing and organising the shows, if there was an accessible space for me at all, it was an afterthought at best. Designated spaces were limited to no more than one companion, and I didn't want to ruin the show for friends when they could be in the crowd with everyone else, so I would either feel guilty or spend the night alone if I chose to use them. I often rejected the segregation even if it meant risking safety and a view of the band.

At one particular show, where the general admission had no designated accessible space, I was forcedly and aggressively removed by multiple large, male members of security, before the band I had come to see even started, for refusing to leave after they dubbed me a 'fire hazard' just for being there with a wheelchair. I kicked up enough of a fuss to get an apology after the fact and free tickets to another show, but my misinformed notions of 'normality' were shattered. No matter how I tried, or how many people overlooked my differences, there were places in the world that I was not welcome.

My perspective changed. The 'compliments' I once gratefully received from people who were miraculously able to look past my disability now felt dismissive. It occurred to me that my disability wasn't something to overcome, that it instead had intrinsically shaped the person I was. It was me and when people rejected that, it felt like they wanted it to go away. They wanted a part of me to go away. I know these people had the best intentions, and at the heart of these statements is an admiration for pushing back against the difficulties that come with having a physical disability. However, it became increasingly hard to navigate those situations where something said from a place of positivity actually began to feel patronising.

I felt the hurt more intensely. In general society, I was used to barriers. Barriers to stores, to restaurants, bars, bathrooms, friends and families' homes, but when it came to music, the cut was deeper. The apathetic shrugs from club owners, tour managers, bouncers and promoters when I enquired about accessibility, left wounds. Friends fiercely defended my right to attend, to experience, and I owe all of them for my not backing down, but it wasn't until later in my life that I really confronted the infinite number of microaggressions as the prejudice that they were.

Though I had been pushing back against them for years, understanding the microaggressions and naming them as such solidified my position and my resolve to change assumptions. I needed to exist in these spaces, to be seen in these spaces unapologetically, in order to be considered for them in the future. The anger and offence towards being excluded from something that was so important to me, a scene that touted itself as a space for everyone, was so easily dismissed as having a 'chip on my shoulder' or an entitlement to more than everyone else, more than I deserved, so I focused the energy into determination, to stake a claim for my space not just at shows, but in the world.

Embracing the fight was liberating. Where I had once quietly accepted the extremes of asexualisation or fetishisation that were blanketed on the disabled community, I allowed myself the same openness that able-bodied friends had, having, enjoying and discussing sex. I worked on accepting the body I had, that didn't, wouldn't and couldn't look like everyone else's, and instead of hiding it under layers of clothing, I covered it in tattoos and put skinny jeans on the legs I had always struggled to accept. I travelled the globe, sometimes with friends, sometimes alone, always looking to prove to myself as well as everyone else that it was for me as much as it was for them. When asked intrusive questions, I no longer felt I owed an explanation. My life, my body, my business was my own.

Life brought me to Toronto, where I worked for a fashion designer. The fashion industry is generally regarded as so removed from 'real life' that it has an entirely new measure of normal, so the fresh challenge of being part of the resistance in this world felt radical to me. While we created custom, couture pieces for film, television and music stars who embodied the almost impossible standard everyone tried to live up to, we also worked on a start-up line of clothing completely redesigned around a seated frame. Clothing that actually looked and felt better for wheelchair users.

I had the privilege of working on projects with some of the industry's most well known models, photographers and publications, and was part of a huge push to bring disability into the mainstream fashion world. Yet, still, simply being on set in this world of manufactured perfection felt like a political act.

This line of work also meant that I received invitations to view designers' launches at Toronto Fashion Week and other major events. More spaces where accessibility rarely, if ever, had to be taken into account in the past. It took a lot of organising but it always worked out that front row was the only place they could make accessible. Something about the visibility of being in one of the fashion world's most coveted spots felt like a statement. My wheelchair and I felt like a huge juxtaposition with the majority of the crowd there, but rather than feel self conscious about the way I stood out and the surprise on people's faces, I was energised and vindicated.

Success to me is no longer 'passing', but standing out. Making a measured difference. Changing attitudes and opinions through being visible, and asking questions that challenge oppression. Carving out a new space through the process of refusing to accept less than inclusion.

It might seem almost extreme, but it is these same antiquated, apathetic 'we don't know where to put you' attitudes in society, that even now see people younger than me in situations not dissimilar to my own, put into nursing homes because there isn't an obvious solution as to where they belong. Integration matters. Everywhere.

Though my able-bodied friends, predominately an exceptional group of women, have and do enable me with their support to contest assumptions and exclusion, the strength and wisdom I have gained from expanding my social circle to include other women with disabilities has been phenomenal. Women like Stella Young, Kelly Vincent, Ing Wong-Ward and Maayan Ziv have given me a sense of powerfulness that continues to grow. I have learned that being offended by exclusion is not a personality flaw or a failing. It's a response to genuine and constant oppression, but it is not the only response.

Being front row on the runway at Toronto Fashion Week is just as important as being front row for a favourite band, as long as we continue to reject the notion that some spaces just can't cater to us.

Prejudice lies at the heart of segregation. My greatest act for change is not retiring to the spaces designated to me by society or, worse yet, retreating or resigning when there are none. I refuse to accept that something that liberates me should also limit me in ways that able-bodied society perpetuates.

THE DIFFICULTY IN BEING GOOD

Zeba Talkhani

When #NastyWomen started trending last year, I couldn't help but smile. In my experience, only an immensely insecure person would call someone nasty. It's not constructive, it doesn't really mean anything and it's a low blow. When there is nowhere to go, you go for nasty. The 2016 election was a difficult one for a lot of us. It was especially difficult for me on account of being a woman, a person of colour and a Muslim. But among all the attacks directed towards people like me, it was the term 'nasty woman' that I kept coming back to.

For as long as I can remember, I wanted to be good. The resurgence of nasty women gave me a chance to reflect on how being called nasty a few years ago would have destroyed me. It also made me wonder where my obsession with 'goodness' come from. And what does being 'good' mean anyway?

My formative years were spent in Saudi Arabia and surrounded by its rich Islamic culture, it was no surprise that I assumed goodness is equal to piety. As I entered my teen years I started reading and learning about Islam in my spare time, away from what was being taught to me in school. During my self-study, I was confronted by one of the most basic principles of Islam: the need to think for ourselves. This is highlighted best when reading the Qur'an. There are numerous verses which are posed as questions rather than instructions such as 'Have you not heard?', 'Will you not consider?', 'Do you not see?' There is also an emphasis on seeking knowledge and learning to glean our own interpretations from the Qur'an. Suddenly, being good meant actively engaging with the religious texts and not passively accepting the established interpretations of others.

Meanwhile, I was also antagonised by the concept of 'honour', the paranoia surrounding women's bodies and the restrictions placed on female mobility, all of which were missing from my reading and understanding of the religious texts. Misogynist interpretations of my religion infiltrated my childhood and the message was clear, 'be good and you will be safe'.

At fourteen, I still aspired to be good, but no longer in the eyes of the people around me. I figured being good meant asking questions, seeking an education and making the most of every opportunity. This realisation, along with a Hadith I read around that time ('verily actions are by intentions, and for every person is what he intended') changed the way I felt about being a Muslim.

Intention is a guiding pillar of Islam. Muslims believe that they are judged for their intentions, not their actions and there is no pressure to prove good intentions to those around us. This knowledge helped me free myself from seeking approval. I no longer needed to be *considered* good to *feel* good about myself. Once I learned to differentiate between haram (religiously prohibited) and aib (culturally inappropriate), I felt more in control of my life. The goal was always to remain Muslim but not to let others use my religion against me.

At seventeen, I moved to India to pursue a BA in Journalism. It was my first time living away from home and in a non-Muslim society. My identity as a Muslim had never been challenged before. Away from home, I found myself unwittingly becoming a spokesperson for my religion and for my life back in Saudi Arabia. Suddenly, it became important for me to have an opinion on everything from extremism in Islam and 9/11 to Shia-Sunni conflicts and women's rights in Saudi Arabia.

Though my faith was always important to me, I had never considered it to be something for others to identify me by and, for the first time, I felt pressured to represent a minority. I felt that my thoughts, my actions and my personal beliefs reflected on others' perception of Islam. I became careful; now it wasn't only about being a good person, it was about being a good Muslim.

It was in this state of mind that I moved to Germany. I had just celebrated my twentieth birthday and I was nervous about being in a country where I didn't speak the language. I also became acutely aware of my vulnerability as a woman. At home, I had never crossed a street on my own and in India I studied in a small campus town where my hostel was a 5-minute walk from my college. When I travelled to neighbouring towns, it was always with friends. For the first time in my life, I was alone.

The fear I had internalised and the stories I had grown up with (all of which can be summarised as 'you will be raped if you aren't good/if you aren't good you deserved to be raped') haunted my time in Germany. One of the reasons given to us in school in support of the veil was that it was there to protect us. That by dressing appropriately we were deterring violence against our bodies. That we were responsible for whatever befell us. At twenty, I revisited this notion because I was scared for myself. I wondered if there was truth in this, if I would feel safer by covering myself.

Being a woman in any part of the world comes with its own kinds of helplessness and it's easy to fall back on misguided notions when scared. Women are constantly being told that we will be safe if we are good. That our worth is in our clothes. How she was dressed still comes up when questioning a rape victim along with her sexual history and the alcohol level in her blood. The message is simple, 'if you are good, we won't hurt you'. But here's the truth: I've never been groped in public since I left home. Unfortunately, I can't say the same about my time in Saudi Arabia.

While I was grappling with being a single woman, I was faced with another reality. I was working late at university one night and needed to catch the last tram back to my accommodation. It was quiet and the streetlights were dim. I started the walk from the station to my room. About halfway there, I ran into a boy I knew from my building. He too was in Germany on an exchange semester.

'Thank God, I ran into you,' I said.

'Why?' he asked.

'I was scared to be walking on my own this late at night,' I replied.

He started laughing.

'What are you scared about? Trust me, they are more scared of you!'

Now it was my turn to ask why.

'Oh, because you are brown,' he replied, as though I was stupid for asking.

I had been so tangled in defining myself as a Muslim and as a woman, I had completely forgotten that I was now also a person of colour in Europe. And there began another journey in trying to define myself, in trying to be good.

I moved to the UK a month before my twenty-first birthday, to pursue my MA. I was used to blatant racism in Saudi Arabia. There were instances of kids as well as grown men rolling down car windows and screaming 'Hindi' at me. It's Arabic for Indian. Being shouted my nationality at me didn't have any impact on how I felt about myself and, I must admit, it didn't offend me. So, it took me a while to realise when someone was being 'politely racist'. I came away from conversations feeling bad but not being able to pinpoint the reason for how I was feeling. It was very frustrating.

When I related these conversations to my friends, I always felt the need to say 'Oh, but I bet she/he didn't mean it like that.' I felt the onus was on me to make sure everyone knew that I'm a good person of colour, that I understand. That I can imagine how difficult it is to be accused of being racist when one was only trying to be nice. To nod and say, 'Yes, yes, we do indeed live in a post-racial world now.'

When I began to stand up for myself or explain my views on Islam/feminism/racism, I was cut short because what I said didn't match the popular narratives. My views didn't count because it was assumed that I didn't know what I was talking about. I once shared a cafeteria table with a guy who felt he could talk over me because he had read an online article about women in Saudi Arabia. I think a lot of people find it difficult to differentiate between projected narratives and personal experiences. I was mistaken when I thought I could make people with bigoted views understand that my personal experiences are true to me and I can't deny them just because it doesn't sit well with their preconceived notions.

The thing about shouting racial slurs from a moving car is that you know exactly what the intentions are. It's to unhinge you, to bully you and to make you feel bad about yourself. But when racism comes wrapped in 'good intentions' it's difficult to pinpoint. It's difficult to share the experiences without being labelled oversensitive or overreaching. Now the pressure was not only to be a good Muslim and a good woman but also a non-judgmental person of colour who doesn't use the 'race card'. Someone 'good white people' can talk to without feeling the pressure to appear non-racist. Got it.

When I share my experiences as a person of colour online, a lot of well-meaning white people write back to me. The messages contain words of advice, most recurring one being 'It's not personal/don't take it personally.' I disagree. It is very personal to my sense of identity, being constantly put on the spot to explain obscure and damaging cultural traditions in Eastern countries, being asked to prove my loyalties and to express my gratefulness for an opportunity to make a living in their country.

There is an acquaintance who can't help but start all his questions to me with 'Do all Muslim women…?' When Trump got elected, he thought it would be funny to joke about how I will no longer be allowed to enter America (while it was already quite disturbing then, it hurt even more following the January 2017 order to temporarily ban citizens from predominantly Muslim countries from entering America). The same acquaintance once overheard a Muslim woman talking about choosing not to take any drugs when giving birth and wanted me to defend this stranger's decision to him. 'Do you think Allah wants you to have labour pains to give you a chance to redeem yourself in his eyes?' The questions don't bother me as much as the sense of entitlement that accompany them. As though I owe this white, educated, middle-class man a response because he chose to engage me in a conversation about my religion. 'Look how open I'm being,' his entitlement says to me. 'Aren't you grateful for this chance to prove your worth to me?', it asks. If I play along, I'm a good immigrant. If I don't engage, I'm refusing to integrate, I'm being a nasty woman.

I first heard the term 'nasty woman' when I was around ten years old and in my opinion it was being used to describe a perfectly normal woman. It was the Urdu version of the term. A young woman was being 'difficult' because she wanted to pursue her career after her wedding. The words were spoken by her potential mother-in-law, in her absence, but in the presence of several other women and me. This woman was proud of her son, who had recently become a doctor. Because of his prestigious career, she had insisted her future daughter-in-law also be a doctor, someone who would understand her son's work commitments. From what I gathered, a matchmaker found her a doctor. Everything was going smoothly until this young woman who invested years of her life in getting an education to become a doctor mentioned that she was indeed going to be one. What a nasty woman!

Since then, references to nasty women have come thick and fast. Girls who don't obey their parents, girls who dress 'provoc-atively', women who are divorced, women who choose to work or hire a nanny. Just women trying to live their lives on their own terms and getting labelled 'nasty' because they chose to not aspire to unrealistic standards set by society.

I'm embarrassed to admit that it took me a long time to

realise that being good is not equal to being subservient. That being good is transient and not worth aspiring to. That being good means different things to different people and it's impossible to please everyone. That pleasing everyone should never be anyone's goal. That being good was not making me happy. In fact, it was making me lose myself. A good woman is not necessarily a happy woman, and I choose happiness above all. Freedom.

THE REST IS DRAG
ONE LESBIAN'S JOURNEY THROUGH BUTCH AND FEMME AND BACK AGAIN

Kaite Welsh

'We're born naked, the rest is drag.' – RuPaul

A strange thing happened in the late 1990s and early 2000s, as lesbian visibility started to creep into mainstream media. The mantle previously held by kd lang and Ellen Degeneres was taken up by Willow and Tara from *Buffy the Vampire Slayer*, the sapphic schoolgirls in Tatu and Britney's MTV liplock with Madonna. When groundbreaking lesbian drama *The L Word* aired, with its scantily-clad cast shot in soft focus for the ads, the message was clear – lezzing it up was finally cool. No longer just the province of tattooed, spiky-haired women in baggy jeans or sportswear – now you could kiss girls and still be pretty – or at least, that value of pretty that still meant white, slim and able-bodied.

As a recently out lesbian looking for love, acceptance and a decent haircut, the messages were somewhat mixed. I spent the next four years veering dramatically between long, Pre-Raphaelite curls and floaty Liberty print dresses and a crew cut accessorised with rainbow hair clips and an eyebrow piercing, never quite sure which made me look more authentically queer.

These days, I'm still not sure. Several years ago, I was at a party with a younger, hipper LGBT crowd when a twenty-something who carried off her eyebrow piercing in a way I never could (perhaps it was the lack of sepsis) claimed she could identify everyone's sexual orientation just by how they were dressed. She made some good guesses – and then she got to me.

'Bisexual' she decided, in a tone that read clearly as 'I'd assume straight but you're in a roomful of queers and I'm trying to be polite.' Maybe she saw the wedding ring and assumed it had been put there by a man, or maybe it was the spectre of femme invisibility rearing its perfectly coiffured head again.

I'd be happy with that – some of my best ex-girlfriends are femmes, after all – if only my sexuality's personal branding was consistent. Entering a bridal shop recently for a bridesmaid's dress fitting, a month later I had to bite my tongue not to explain my awkwardness, unshaved legs and zero clue as to what would 'suit' me with, 'Sorry, I'm a lesbian. We don't really do this sort of thing.' No matter all the girls in white dresses marrying each other, my queerness is still a handy explanation for why some aspects of traditional womanhood completely pass me by. It's not that I think high heels inherently oppress women, I just can't bloody walk in them. That level of normalised hyperfemininity, the kind that goes unnoticed by the general populace because primped, primed and hairless is how we've come to expect women, sits so at odds with who I am, it feels like an outsize fancy dress costume. It's not even drag, because drag is about creativity, power, redesigning yourself and saying 'fuck you' to gender roles.

So why do I still not feel – or feel like I look – queer enough? With my wedding ring and my ticking biological clock, with my column in a right wing establishment newspaper, maybe I've got some kind of heteronormative Stockholm Syndrome. Binding my breasts so that my shirt buttons neatly, slicking my hair back with Topman pomade lets me pass, takes the ways in which I conform to society's expectations and turns it into a political statement.

In a Telegraph article from late 2015, I wrote 'after decades of being super feminine, I'm tapping into my inner dapper butch and feeling gorgeous … In a dress I pass for straight, at least until you start talking to me. But like this, in polished brogues, chunky leather jewellery and a half Windsor knotted at my neck, my sexuality is inescapable. This is comfort, to me. This is smart, suave, dapper, and I don't care if all those words are normally associated with men because I look really good. And I feel good, because the secret is that these clothes are designed to flatter everybody. Literally, every body – put on a dinner jacket and you can't help but channel a bit of 007, and I was never meant to be a Bond Girl. But dress like this long enough, and you learn to spot the signs, the flicker of annoyance from men in T-shirts and jeans that I'm out-dressing them, wearing their clothes and doing it better.'

Fastforward a year and I'm in a dress that gives me Jessica Rabbit curves, standing in front of a mirror and thinking 'This. Maybe this is it.' But once it's paid for, it still feels like a costume. It's like I'm constantly trying to find my default setting, the one where I get dressed in the morning and don't realise part way through the day that I've come out in the wrong costume, Superman when I should be Clark Kent.

I thought, one hot Friday in July, that I'd find the answer if I started from scratch, undoing the thirtysomething years of struggling to find an identity that sat comfortably between boy and girl, butch and femme, scrappy Northern dyke and power lesbian with cut glass vowels. When I shaved my head, I felt like a blank canvas, one on which I could finally paint on the right look. I walked out to buy the brightest pink lipstick I could find and tweeted a selfie. 'You look like a fierce queen' a friend texted. I didn't ask which kind she meant. I spent six months alternately playing with a makeup palette that would make a showgirl proud and wearing hoodies that made me look like a teenage boy. I scrawled on eyeliner mustaches, wore velvet turbans, got called 'sir' and was asked if I was having a Britney-style breakdown. What I hadn't factored in was the fact that short hair requires considerably more upkeep – not just going to the hairdressers every six weeks, but remembering to make an appointment and then making the appointment and then actually remembering to fucking attend. Some of the most high maintenance people I know are somewhere on the butch spectrum. Long hair only requires remembering where I put my one hair clip and trying to trim my fringe in a straight-ish line with the kitchen scissors.

Of course, these days even our subcultures have subcultures. Autostraddle, a lifestyle website aimed at queer women, sells T-shirts with a variety of labels. Am I actually just a 'lazy femme'? Maybe I should forget the labels altogether and just buy the boxer shorts they sell with a coy pair of scissors printed on the front. I don't want to reduce my sexuality and gender to fit some consumerist tick box and I don't think that anyone's identity fits on a T-shirt – although look at this rack, you can't say there isn't room – but there's something incredibly lonely about seeing so many options that still don't feel right.

Butch, femme and the whole spectrum in between is about so much more than clothes – historically, they were roles that signified something about your personality, something that mirrored traditional straight gender roles but with the added fun of getting the option of throwing off your original programming for something new. And of course, they signified who fucked and who got fucked. Even now, when we're long past making assumptions about who does what in the bedroom based on haircuts, the saying still lingers for women who shift between boundaries in a certain way – 'butch in the streets, femme in the sheets.' My wife has a T-shirt that says 'Dorothy in the streets and Blanche in the sheets,' which makes much more sense to me. Maybe I should just define my gender presentation by fictional characters – Q in the streets (nerdy, rocks a parka), 007 in the sheets (arrogant, overly reliant on gadgets).

There's a term in BDSM – a switch. It means you can go from bottom/submissive to top/domme, and that's the closest I've come in the Venn diagram between sexuality and fashion that I've been circling for most of my adult life. Soft butch, hard femme – I'm a human Pinterest board, filing away images and aesthetics and planning to try them out when I have a gap in my schedule, which is never. Maybe I should embrace the ambiguity. Maybe I should divide my wardrobe into butch and femme – or Rachel Maddow and *The L Word*'s Bette Porter.

If my relationship to queer fashion can be summed up in a song lyric, it's Jenny Lewis crooning mournfully, 'You are what you love, not what loves you back.' There have been huge swathes of my life where clothes were an annoyance, a social necessity. Not because I was tempted by nudism – for heaven's sake I'm British, with all the inhibitions and rain that implies – but because my body felt like an irrelevance. Even now, I often say I'd rather be a brain in a jar without all the messy, breakable nonsense that comes with actual humanity. Ageing throws a spanner in the works – where once my tweed made me look dapper, like a 1920s Sapphic spinster, now I just look like I live in the Home Counties and vote Conservative. So now, between the side of me that wants glitter and swirling skirts and the side of me that wants tailored suits and pocket squares, I have to navigate the self that longs for Boden and Barbour and gets her fashion advice from Mumsnet.

But in rediscovering the ways I can present my physical form to the world, I'm learning to love it again. Gone are the too-tight jeans that compress my soft tummy into something vaguely acceptable beneath a flowing top – if I want to show that extra tyre I'm carrying around I will, all that extra fat will come in handy once society descends even further into dystopia anyway. I get to decide what my body means, what it looks like. I get to decide if I announce my queerness from a distance – there are days it can be seen from space, especially when I get that half Windsor knot right – or if I want to keep it lurking under the surface like the Loch Ness Monster in a pretty dress, ready at any minute to disturb the tranquil surface and subvert your expectations.

THE DARK GIRL'S ENLIGHTENMENT

Joelle A. Owusu

Chocolate. Ebony. Brownie. Nubian Queen. Blackie. Negress. Girrrrl. Sassy (with accompanying finger snaps). Sista. Feisty. Fierce. Coconut/Bounty/Oreo (Black on the outside, but white on the inside). Black bitch. Aggressive. Jungle Bunny. Secret Bloke. Monkey. Ratchet. Ghetto Girl. Gorilla.

These words lined up together are not random and the people who know this all too well are the people they are aimed at: Black women. From an extremely early age, I quickly learned that society had already formed an opinion of me, my skin and my future before I could. Being born with the extremely rare amalgamation of a vagina and dark skin guaranteed a lifetime of navigating through the political minefield that was being a Black girl in a world that wished you didn't exist.

The first time I was called a monkey was in Year Two of primary school. A white boy in my year prodded my back during assembly and announced it whilst making accompanying arm gestures. Despite being only seven, I knew exactly what he meant, but laughed it off because he was 'just joking around'. Even at that age, I knew that retaliating or telling a grown up would have little effect. So I buried the hurt.

Being the only Black kid in the year came with that struggle, and being a little girl who didn't want to be called a 'cry baby' also stopped me from speaking out to teachers. However, it was the same teachers who tried their hardest to force me into track and field sports, when all I wanted to do was read books about science and dig for fossils in my garden. My mother fought back against them and won, without me even realising what was going on. Now I understand, although this was also around the time I moved to the more affluent Surrey country and managed to subconsciously change my accent from a South London twang. At ten, I truly believed that nailing that perfect 'posh phone voice' would possibly put me in a better position in life – miles ahead of my inner London Black counterparts.

I am now in Year Eight or Nine, studying the Transatlantic Slave Trade. A girl, whom I considered a friend turned to me and whispered *'your ancestors were my ancestors' slaves'*. She said it so delicately and so softly, without an ounce of remorse and, because of that, it ate me up more than I let on. But I supressed the hurt like an obedient darkie.

I don't know why I decided to take her outside our classroom and confront her two years later, but my soul rejoiced even when my body was consumed by fear. Fear of looking like an angry Black girl with a chip on her shoulder, who was harassing an innocent rosy-cheeked student. As expected, she denied everything and I looked bitter and Black, boisterous and Black, beastly and Black.

I am now in my early twenties, hundreds of miles away from the London bubble. I'm so far north in Scotland that pretty much everyone who asks me where I'm from is either shocked that I'm not a Nigerian international student or a Saaaf London ex-gang member.

I'm clutching onto my friend's arms for dear life as we stumble over cobbles and potholes to get to a nightclub. My group, made out of mainly Black girlfriends, were sometimes harassed by drunken Scottish men shouting 'Niggers! Run! The KKK's coming for ye!' How inventive. What's interesting is that the same type of men would grab my hips and pinch my bum before dissolving away into the crowd of clubbers. A week later, they'd mix it up by grinding up against me, taking not-so-candid pictures of my bum and almost twisting my arm out of the socket whilst trying to drag me to the bar. They'd then offend my sinuses with their boozy breath and invite me back to theirs, mistaking me for some exotic creature from the African wilderness.

These men of various races felt entitled to touch my hair, waist and arse, but when I showed any form of resistance, they called me ugly – someone who should be grateful for getting attention from them. They failed to tick me off their weird sexual bucket list and so made sure I paid for it with humiliating insults. I fractured their fragile masculinity as they failed to claim first prize of fucking a foreign-looking chick. Their dreams of retelling the incredible fable twenty years later in the pub to their glassy-eyed mates were dashed by a 'bloke in a wig'. At this point, all I can do is send my sincerest apologies and, being on the generous side, I am more than willing to accept invoices to pay for the restoration of all the egos I damaged.

Did all of this happen back in the 1970s and 80s, when blatant racism and misogyny were practically the norm in Europe? No, my friend, these were all 21st century incidents that left a young girl angry, confused and struggling to find her place in a world that seemed to hate her.

It was clear that my dark skin, bushy hair and curvy body did not fit the typical standard of beauty: pale and slim. The more I admired icons like Serena Williams and Michelle Obama for all their successes, the more I noticed the hatred towards them – simply for being Black women in the spotlight, a space usually reserved for white women. They are constantly referred to as 'men' and 'apes' – anti feminine, ugly and wild.

As I got older, taunts became less subtle and more complex. The insults were disguised as compliments, but still tried to reinforce the fact that I was an 'Other' in a world where people who looked like them owned the culture and therefore got to define beauty standards. 'You're really well-spoken,' was a sentence I heard a lot, which I knew really meant 'you're Black, you're meant to speak only in "street" slang.'

'Can I touch your hair?' is my personal favourite, meaning, 'What are these exotic wires that grow out of your scalp? What kind of witchcraft is this?' But at least they asked, unlike others who felt it necessary to poke and prod me as if I were an animal in a lab. *Mate, am I a pan-Asian buffet? Am I a 70s funk track? I'm not to be sampled or used in your social experiment because, believe it or not, I was put on this earth to be much more than that.*

'You're so pretty... you know... for a Black girl.' – used by boys of all races, but also as a reminder that I should be grateful for their compliment, 'cause... you know, I'm a Black girl, who needs to know that she is at the bottom of the pretty pyramid – bottom rung of the Ladder of Likability.

Crowd favourite 'Don't make everything about race!' often followed by the classic 'I don't see race' was the last straw for me. This was misogynoir, a term coined by Black feminist Moya Bailey that refers to the specific type of discrimination that is directed at Black women. I couldn't bear taking on yet another label, but for some reason, it brought me comfort because, for the first time in over a decade, I realised that I was not alone in my experiences.

I was so used to laughing away the pain and frustration because as soon as I showed discomfort, I would be seen as an Angry Black Woman: the mother of all misogynoir stereotypes. We all know the connotations: the loud-mouthed, neck snapping, finger clicking, 'independent' woman. And even when I didn't fit any of the stereotypes, it confused people.

I didn't realise how much I was crumbling under a stranger's opinion of me. I was judged and hated for simply existing – for taking up space which apparently I did not deserve. I tried to fight back by emphasising how much I loved music that wasn't rap or hip-hop and always making sure my frizzy natural hair was hidden from view under a weave made from the hair of strangers in Asia. I also became conscious of what I wore: no hoodies, sweatpants or flashy jewellery in public, in case strangers thought I'd approach them to sell my latest mixtape.

I made sure I showed absolutely no emotion and stayed away from any political debates or current affairs discussions outside of my home. Supressing my feelings was easier than being seen as a Black girl with an 'attitude' for expressing emotion and passion. As a result of this, my mental health and relationships suffered.

During my late teens, I discovered Feminism and thought I had finally found a place to belong. I read about the fearless Suffragettes in the UK, Second Wave activists and radical feminists of 60s America, but something was missing. Where were the Black women? Were they not involved in the fight for women's liberation? I thought further about the role of Black women in the UK and realised that we had been completely written out of the British narrative, so had no choice but to cling on to the American one, although we are not the same people.

The lack of dark women who looked like me in magazines reinforced the notion that I wasn't worthy enough to demand regular feminine things in my shade like makeup, flesh coloured bras, tights or plasters. Even today, one pair of brown tights would set me back twenty pounds and I still have to shop high-end for the right foundation.

I have supressed and policed my own emotions so much that simply tweeting or writing about my experiences is seen as a radical act – a rude outburst that ruffles the feathers of the privileged majority, who dismiss anything and everything I say as delusion. Cute counter-narratives call me paranoid, as if I cannot possibly be an expert in my own experiences. I class myself as an expert because I have been in this invol-untary, unpaid job since birth. For twenty-four hours, seven days a week and with no time off, so I know what the fuck I'm talking about. They ask for facts and statistics and claim victory when I can only pour out my feelings in a sea of uncomfortable anecdotes.

'Not everything is about race.'

'Not everything is sexist.'

Perhaps not. But enough of it is for it to be an ongoing problem that we simply cannot sweep under the carpet anymore. Being dark *and* female has made me hyperaware of nonsense, insults and abuse targeted at me and if I want change, I have to fight for it and write about it. Women like me are on the receiving end of both bigotries, so big congratulations for proudly proclaiming that you 'don't see race' and that 'men and women are completely equal in this day and age'. It's great that *you* are privileged enough to never have to deal with both issues, so you can just speak it out of existence and deny misogynoir.

There is this feeling that it's impossible to be a bigoted feminist because as women, we experience ignorance, hate crimes and discrimination as a collective. But we as Black women are still not allowed to showcase our entire emotional spectrum. Black women in western countries still face two extremes: rejection due to our skin tone and features and/or fetishised and objectified because of it. But even on the African continent, some Black women turn to skin bleaching to remove the melanin in their skin – light is right, Black is whack.

And as feminists growing up in this digital age, (where anyone with a Twitter account thinks their opinion is fact), we have the added pressure of having to explain how and why we are not the enemy of men and how the feminist ideal works for everyone. But without *all* women being included in the wide and varied spectrum, the fight for equality is useless.

No one in the western world seemed to believe racism actually existed in the 21st century until Donald Trump won the Presidential election in 2016. The only people who didn't seem surprised were minorities, especially Black women. We watched, with our eyes rolling back into our heads as the tears of safety pin-wearing white feminists flooded the web. The public detestation of anyone beyond beige had been placed in the centre of global politics for the entire world to see and all these women could not believe what had happened. These women, who proudly proclaim to be intersectional feminists in their Twitter bios, had had their eyes closed and mouths shut for years, whilst Black women tried to tell them their truths.

Black women don't need 'white saviours' who think they're

helping by saying 'I'd love a curvy body like yours' or 'You're not being discriminated against. We live in a meritocracy, so just work harder.' No. We need allies. We need support, we need you to acknowledge your white privilege and we *need* to be believed when we open up about the shit we've had to deal with our whole lives.

If all those things are too hard for you to accept and put into practice, then you are not an intersectional feminist, wanting equality for all women, regardless of race, sexual orientation, class, etc., and if you are not an intersectional feminist then you are not a feminist at all. Remove your badge and hang it up for someone else to use because the battle for equality will only ever be but half won.

So, where am I now in 2017?

I have just turned twenty-three, but I am tired – now exhausted of policing myself, my emotions and my looks just to make strangers around me comfortable. I have come to realise that my Blackness is a blessing and my sense of womanhood is also a blessing. But in spite of all this, I am Black before I am a person and I am Black before I am a woman. I tried for so long to put my Blackness and womanhood on the same level, but I know that they are both marginalised and not equal.

Everyone and their second cousin's dog seems to have an opinion on a Black woman's hair, her accent, her choice of partner, her profession and then berate her for being anything outside of their world of labels and insults. But I will tell you this: this will be the last time I write about it and this will be the last time you close your ears to anyone who doesn't look like you.

The way I style my hair is not up for debate.

My body and my accent is not up for debate.

My beautiful Black Britishness is certainly not up for debate.

My existence is not up for debate.

I am Black, I am a woman and I am British. I am proud of all three, whilst being fully aware that I will always be seen as an 'Other'. I am proud of that too because never fully being on the inside allows me to notice indifference. I am always watching and am ready to challenge the injustices that plague our great nation. I have also learned that encouraging friends to branch out of their comfortable, cultural bubble is the truest form of freedom. It is the only way we, as women, can finally shatter that glass ceiling trapping us and that glass floor stopping marginalised women from rising with us.

Black British women have been invisible for too long. Absent from feminist discussion, and ignored from race and culture debates. No more. We are now occupying space that was not created for us, but there is plenty of room to fill with our thoughts, work and opinions, which are just as valid as anyone else's. Black girls like me will no longer write in whispers and we will no longer survive in shadows. Our melanin may be magic, but it cannot be kept in the cold.

The world is a dangerous place right now, but not as dangerous as a nasty woman with a pen in her hand and story to tell. These voices telling our truths cannot be shaken and they certainly will not be drowned out any more.

Why fear us when you can join us?

BIOGRAPHIES

Ren Aldridge is an artist, musician and writer. She fronts feminist hardcore punk band Petrol Girls who released their debut album *Talk of Violence* in November 2016. Ren completed her BA Fine Art at Goldsmiths in 2013 where she was Women's Officer on the Students Union. All of Ren's creative output involves words and symbols, from large scale text sculptures to textile poems; lyric writing to zines. Being involved in feminist and other forms of activism has inspired her increasingly to write.
www.renaldridge.co.uk
www.petrolgirls.bandcamp.com

Sim Bajwa is a sales assistant/admin assistant/writer living in Edinburgh. She graduated from Edinburgh Napier with an MA in Creative Writing in 2016. Her work has previously been featured in Fictionvale Magazine and Helios Quarterly, and she is currently working on her first fantasy novel. Her favourite things are nail polish, chocolate, and cats.

Sasha de Buyl-Pisco is a writer and illustrator based in Edinburgh. From Belgium by way of an extended stint in Ireland, she writes short stories and makes comics. You can find her on Twitter at @sashadebuyl and keep up to date with her work on www.sashadebuylpisco.com

Rowan C. Clarke studied political sciences and human rights in Italy and France before moving to the UK. Rowan works in publishing and is currently researching a book on bravery. She lives in Scotland with her wife, pets and overfilled bookshelves.

Biographies

Kristy Diaz (@diazzzz) is a communications professional and music writer based in Leicester, via the USA. She is a contributor at Track 7 and Upset Magazine, as well as a number of DIY zines. She graduated with a BA in Arts Management in 2008 and has been a passionate supporter of independent music for many years as a DJ, label co-founder and fan. Her interests include intersectional feminism and left-wing politics, supporting the Leicester Riders basketball team, and hanging out with her cat.

Laura Jane Grace is the singer and songwriter behind the band, Against Me!. Her memoir *Tranny: Confessions of Punk Rock's Most Infamous Anarchist Sellout* is out now, published by Hachette.

Claire L. Heuchan writes as the award-winning blogger Sister Outrider, covering themes such as intersectional feminism, race in the feminist movement, and Black feminist praxis. She is a freelance writer and feminist workshop facilitator – sharing ideas is her passion. In her spare time Claire volunteers for Glasgow Women's Library and is a member of the Scottish Queer International Film Festival committee.

Aside from writing, activism, and getting salty on Twitter (@ClaireShrugged), Claire researches Black feminists' use of digital media in activism. Claire is a PhD candidate at the University of Stirling, where she attained her MLitt in Gender Studies.

Elise Hines is a 20-year veteran of the world of Information Technology, an accomplished Technical Communicator, and, at times, a concert photographer. She's a native of New York City and currently resides in Raleigh, North Carolina.

Becca Inglis wants to be the girl with the most cake. She is an Edinburgh-based writer who regularly reviews theatre and poetry for TV Bomb, with a special focus on women writers and artists. She has previously been published in the Dangerous Women Project and blogged for Hollaback!, Linguisticator, and Lunar Poetry. Becca has branched out into other female musicians since discovering Hole ten years ago, but Courtney Love is still the reason that she bleaches her hair.

Nadine Aisha Jassat is the author of *Still*, a poetry pamphlet exploring women's stories and women's survival. She has performed solo shows at the Edinburgh Fringe Festival, the Just Festival, and the Audacious Women Festival, and was the first Writer in Residence for YWCA Scotland – The Young Women's Movement. Nadine works in the movement to end gender-based violence, and has worked with young people to create theatre exploring sexual violence. She delivers feminist creative writing workshops and is currently focusing on creative participation with young women of colour exploring sexism, racism and Islamophobia.

Jonatha Kottler is from Albuquerque, NM where she was a lecturer in the Honors College at The University of New Mexico. She moved with her husband, son, and three very well-traveled cats from the USA to Amsterdam before falling head over heels in love with Edinburgh. She is a happy member of Edinburgh's Write Like A Grrrl community and runs a reading and writing group for the local charity ECAS. She read a piece at Story Shop at the Edinburgh International Book Festival in August 2016 and recently contributed to the Dangerous Women Project. She is currently completing her first novel.

Laura Lam was born in the late eighties and raised near San Francisco, California, by two former Haight-Ashbury hippies. After studying literature and creative writing at university, she relocated to Scotland to be with her husband. Her first book, *Pantomime*, the first book in the Micah Grey series, was released in 2013, which was a Scottish Book Trust Teen Book of the Month, won the Bisexual Book Award, was listed a Top Ten Title for the American Library Association List, and was nominated for several other awards. The sequel, *Shadowplay*, followed in 2014, as well as the Vestigial Tales, self-published short stories and novellas set in the same world. The third book in the series, *Masquerade*, will follow in 2017. Her latest book is *False Hearts*, a near-future thriller released in June 2016 by Tor/Macmillan. She is still hiding from sunshine in Scotland and writing more stories.

Jen McGregor is an Edinburgh-based writer and director. She works mostly in theatre with occasional forays into fiction, poetry and other forms of writing. She blogs about mental health, arts politics and whatever else catches her attention at jenmcgregor.com.

Her recent work includes '#SonsOfGod: Vox', a futuristic adaptation of Coriolanus that is currently touring Italy, 'Volante', a play about an 18th century rope dancer currently in development with Fronteiras Theatre Lab, and 'Unfinished Demon Play', which was written with guidance from Rob Drummond under Playwrights' Studio Scotland's mentoring scheme.

Katie Muriel is a 20-something mixed Latinx chick, rabid intersectional feminist, writer, and future cat lady. She is also a university student with an A.A.S. degree in criminal justice who is currently working toward a Bachelors in criminology. The goal is victim advocacy, but for the moment, she is mainly focused on school and how many seasons of any given show she can feasibly marathon on Netflix in a single day. The word 'bibliophile' is her favorite identifier and she's positive she'll never have enough bookshelves.

Biographies

Christina Neuwirth was born in Austria and now lives in Edinburgh. Her short fiction has been published in Gutter and 404 Ink. Christina has written and directed short films, performed at the Scottish International Storytelling Festival and produced and written zines. Her novella *Amphibian* was shortlisted for the 2016 Novella Award, and she is currently working on her first novel.

Belle Owen has spent a large portion of her life traveling and living all over the world, recently returning home to Adelaide, Australia after 2.5 years in Toronto, where she worked in marketing and social media for a fashion designer, running an accessible brand. When she isn't scouring the world for vegan treats, she is writing on a freelance basis about music, entertainment and accessibility issues. Belle is a strong advocate for social change and accessibility awareness, and often discusses these issues in her writing, presentations and online presence. Her work projects have been featured by Vice, Harper's Bazaar, Fashionista.com, Notable.ca, Huffington Post and refinery 29.

Joelle Owusu is a Surrey-based writer who currently works in publishing. She recently graduated from the University of Aberdeen with a BSc in Petroleum Geology. As a staunch advocate for intersectional feminism, she is committed to helping others acknowledge, accept and embrace their individuality. As a way of encouraging young people (especially People of Colour) to open up about their mental health, she self-published her diary, *Otherness* in October 2016. @joelle_o.

Chitra Ramaswamy is an award winning journalist and writer. Her first book, *Expecting*, a collection of nine essays for the nine months of pregnancy and birth, was published in April 2016 by Saraband. It won the Saltire First Book of the Year award and has been described as 'immediately, poignantly, gripping... magnificent' by Zoe Williams, 'elegant, funny, brimming with acute observations and suffused with a gentle intimacy' by Gavin Francis, and 'a glorious read' by Denise Mina. She currently writes mainly for The Guardian and lives in Edinburgh with her partner, young son, and rescue dog.

Mel Reeve lives in Glasgow with two dogs. She works as an archivist and recently graduated with an MSc from the University of Glasgow. In her spare time she writes, makes music, recently self-published a zine of poetry and photography, and runs an online shop selling jewellery and clothes of her own design.
@melreeve

Zeba Talkhani is a writer and production editor with an interest in identity, feminism, intersectionality and social deconstruction. @zebatalk

Alice Tarbuck is a writer and researcher based in Edinburgh. She is completing a PhD on poet and visual artist Thomas A. Clark. Recent publications appear in Dangerous Women, Antiphon, Zarf and Three Drops from the Cauldron. She is part of Edinburgh writers collective *content work produce form*. She is on Twitter: @atarbuck

Laura Waddell is a graduate of the University of Glasgow with an MLitt in Modernities and works as a publishing professional. As a freelance literary publicist specialising in translation her clients have included Les Fugitives, CB Editions, and Calisi Press, and formerly, Marketing Manager of Freight Books. She is also a Board Member of PEN Scotland and creator of poetry newsletter Lunchtime Poetry. As a writer of articles, criticism, and fiction, she has been published in *The Digital Critic* (OR Books, 2017), the Independent, Sunday Mail, 3:AM, Gutter, Glasgow Review of Books, Bella Caledonia, Libertine, TYCI, and Parallel magazine.

Kaite Welsh is an author, critic and journalist living in Scotland. Her novel *The Wages of Sin*, a feminist historical crime novel set in Victorian Edinburgh, is out from Headline in June 2017.

Her fiction has featured in several anthologies and she writes a regular column on LGBT issues for the Daily Telegraph as well as making frequent appearances on BBC Radio 4's Woman's Hour. In 2014 she was shortlisted for both the Scottish New Writers Award and the Moniack Mhor Bridge Award. She has also been shortlisted for the 2010 Cheshire Prize for Fiction and the 2010 Spectrum Award for short fiction.

A NOTE FROM THE EDITORS

The idea for *Nasty Women* came about, probably unsurprisingly, the day after Donald J. Trump was voted President Elect of the United States of America on 8th November 2016. We wanted to do something to stand against this, and as a new publisher, it felt like a book was our own small answer to say 'Enough is enough'.

Within four weeks of the vote this book was fully commissioned, after ten it grasped worldwide attention through the successful Kickstarter campaign and within seventeen it was published. A project of uncompromising speed and volume, *Nasty Women* is a response to and a voice against the dangerous normalisation of right-leaning hatred that currently poisons media across the globe.

The project was fully funded in three days, and ended on 369% after the full thirty days across January of 2017. For one, this left us ecstatic that we could share these stories with you, but more so we felt it was proof that in an age of 'post-truths' and 'alternative facts' (or as they're better known: lies) that real experience still matters to many.

By now you'll have read accounts on what it is to be a woman from over 20 incredible contributors (if you haven't – why are you reading us babbling away at the end? Go back, and read the rest of this later. We're not important) and hopefully learned something new between these pages. This collection sought to showcase just a snapshot of the diversity in experience of being a woman today, and open peoples' eyes in some way. We ourselves as the editors learned so much more than we expected in reading and working on these essays, even though we knew (or thought we knew) what to expect within each issue that's touched upon. We have barely skimmed the surface in *Nasty Women*, but this powerful collection is one we hope to expand on in the (likely turbulent) years to come.

So what next? Well, for 404 Ink, our mission is to continue to give platforms to new voices. For as long as this American administration is in power and rolling back fundamental human rights, exacerbating hateful divides and making the world a dangerous place for so many, and governments comfortably sit in their pockets, we'll publish real stories and do our bit to stand against the hate. *Nastier Women? Nastiest Women?* Who knows what form they'll exist in, but it's going to happen. They won't stop, and neither will we.

As for you, we hope you've seen the power in real stories. Those who shout loudest at 3am on Twitter currently shape what's 'true' regardless of reality and so the onus is on others to shout back. We're two loud Scots, and we're using our platform to help others shout back in their own way. We hope you'll feel more confident to tell your own stories, or join us in boosting the voices of others, and keep pushing back.

Keep telling your stories.

And tell them loud.

WITH THANKS

to the backers who made *Nasty Women* possible (and those who wish to remain anonymous):

@kayjoon
A E J Kimmons
Aaron Gilmore
Aaron O'Dowling-Keane
Abbie Headon
Abigail Houseman
Acacia Ives
Addison Vada
Adrian Todd Zuniga
Adriana Becerra
Aija Oksman
Aileen Appleyard
Aileen McKay
Ailie Crerar
Aimie West
Aims G
Aislin CJ Le Galloudec
Aisling McGing
Alex Burton-Keeble
Alex Palermo
Alex Peterson
Alex Simotes
Alex Toor
Alex Viccars
Alexa Radcliffe-Hart
Alexandra Maria Johanna
    Zimmermann
Alexandra McCourt

Alexia Richardson
Ali Easton
Ali George
Alice Bremner Watt
Alice Fischer
Alice Hobbs
Alice Laing
Alicia Duffy
Alicia Soshi Tan
Alicia Thorpe
Alicja Tokarska
Alisa Roser
Alisa Wylie
Alison Baker
Alison Belsham
Alison Sakai
Alison Savage
Alistair Braidwood
Allison Laasch
Allison Strachan
Ally Crockford
Ally Shwed
Amanda Bell
Amanda Fairey
Amanda Gernentz Han
Amanda Grace Sweet
Amanda Stanley (TYCI)
Amanda Tillman

These people...

Amber Kirk-Ford
Amie Jordan
Amos How
Ampy Dhillon
Amy Bruhl
Amy Dickenson
Amy Elizabeth Hill
Amy Lawson
Amy Louise Blaney
Amy Louise Hendry
Amy St Johnston
Amy Taylor
Amy Wong
Ana-Isabel Nölke
Anastasija Mezecka
Andi Anderson
Andrea Clark
Andrea Lupien
Andrew Noel
Andrew Sample
Angela Atkinson
Angela Docherty
Angela Hatcher
Angela Jackson
Aniessa
Ann Marie C Pfohl
Anna Balogh
Anna BristowM.
Anna Hauschild
Anna Herzog
Anna Mack
Anna-Lisa Doyle
Anna-Marie Fitzgerald
Annalisa King
Anne Sutherland, MD

Anne-Gwenn
Anne-Marie Mackin
Annie King
Anniken Blomberg
Anouk Vos
Aran Ward Sell
Archana Murthy
Ardie Collins
Ariel Du
Ariëlla Reinders
Arlene Finnigan
Arusa Qureshi
Ashley B.
Ashley McGregor Dey
Ashley Orndorff
Astlyr
Asuka Fuji
Aurora Brunvoll
Aurora Green
Automated Luxury
(Clare Robertson)
Autumn Aurelia
Ava Adler
Avon Ewens
Barb Kuntova
Barbara Chaplin
Barbara McVeigh
Bärbel McRitchie
Bear Weiter
Beat Geissler
Bec Evans
Becca Bunce
Becca Inglis
Becca Pirie
Becci Hutchins

Becki Cardosi
Becky Kate Hall
Bekah Wightman
Benjamin Bisset
Berenice Jasper
Beth Braun
Beth Cardier
Beth Cochrane
Beth MCDXXIX Beiter
Beth Morris
Beth O'Rafferty
Beth Smout
Beth Vanson
Bethanie Short
Bethany Lamont
Bex Hughes
Bill Cannon
biomechanoid
Blaise Marshall
Bonnie Bertram
Bonnie McLeish
Brandon Chappell
Brandon D'Orlando
Brandon Lienau
Brendan Freehart
Brianna Vincent
Bridgette
Briony Cullin
Britta Helm
Bryan Mutai
Bryce Coefield
Brysen Bristow
CaffeinatedOwl9
Caitie-Jane Cook
Caitlin & Nora

Callum Sharp
camb1125@gmail.com
Cameron Foster
Cara Rainbow
Cara Vescio
Carissa A Clohessy
Carlotta Eden
Carly Elizabeth Howar
Carly M. Bennett
Carly Marilyn Flood
Caroline Blake
Caroline Callaghan
Caroline Gillett
Caroline Goldsmith
Caroline Grebbell
Caroline Kavanagh
Caroline Vass
Carolyn Black
Carrie Hitt
Cas Sewell-Storey
Casey McKenzie
Casondra Brewster
Cassandra Sandquist
Cassie Fox
Cat Clarke
Cat Ziemak
Catherine Desia Bolt
Catherine Harker
Catherine Simpson
catherine_webb1996@
hotmail.com
Cathryn Steele
Catriona M Cox
Caz Saramowicz
Chad Appenzeller

These people…

Charlène Busalli
Charley Hemmings
Charlie Morris
Charlott Schönwetter
Charlotte Bence
Charlotte Broadley
Charlotte Duff
Charlotte, Chloe & Leah…
All Classy, Nasty Women.
Chelsea Yarbro
Cheryl Lyman
Chiara Bullen
Chiara Mac Call
Chiara Montresor
Chloe McLeod
Chris & Caitlin Grieves
Chris Baldie
Chris Mandalov
Chris McQueer
Chris Scott
Christin Zirkelbach
Christina Buch-Petersen
Christina Stead
Christina Wenig
Christine Evans
Christine Staley Corr
Christine Wilson
Ciara Daly
Cindy Powell
Cio Dav
Claire Askew
Claire Dean
Claire Evans
Claire Forknell
Claire Genevieve

Claire H. Evans
Claire Himsworth
Claire J Furey
Claire Louise
Claire Maxwell
Claire O'Gallagher
Claire Querée
Claire Squires
Claire Stewart
Claire Westwood
Clare Archibald
Clare Cavanagh
Clare Jane Hewitt
Clare M
Clarissa Widya
Clémence
Colleen Elizabeth
Colleen Moens
Coral Williamson
creativebloch.com
Cristin Newkirk-Thompson
Crystal and Courtney Collins
Cynthia Estelle Jones
Cynthia Kreitz
D Franklin
D Morton
Daiden O'Regan
Daniel Hird
Danielle Karthauser
Danielle Lowe
Dan Dalton
Danniella Josephine
Daphne van de Burgwal
Daphne Koumpa
Darren Lipman

Dave Coates
Dave Fraser
Dave McNicol
Dave n Pat
Dave Rowlinson
David Contreras Medi
David R Brook
Dayle Fyock
Dead Ink Books
Dear Damsels
Debbie Cannon
Debbie Hannan
Debbie Prior
Deborah Roden
Debra
Dee McNicol
Delia Poon
Denyse Beaulieu
Dhev Raj Tamang
Dhruv Sapra
Diane Stewart
Diljeet Kaur Bhachu
Dinah Davis
Domenic Sherony
Dominika Jackowska
Dominique J.
Donette Bisbee
Donna Kean
Doris Lanz
Dorothy Nicholson
Dory Ferguson
Douglas Jones
Dr Doris Ruth Eikhof
Dr Joana Vassilopoulou
Dr PJ Naylor

Dr. Andrea Clark, PhD
Dr. Bushra Anjum
Dr. Heiko Kulinna
DSCW
Dyan Muijsenberg
E H Young
Eda Ulus
Edmee Sierts
Eileen Whelan
Eilidh Lean
Eimear Hurley
Eimear O' Carroll
eivipop
Eleanor Smith
Elena Morgan
Eley Williams
Elina Kyriazi
Elise Beek
Elise Hines
Elisha Leavy
Elizabeth Jackson
Elizabeth Reeder
Elizabeth Stanley
Ella Evans
Ellen Davies
Ellie Hughes
Ellis Griffiths
Elodie Saccoccio
Eloise McAllister
Elspeth Forbes
Emerald Stacy
Emilie Chambeyron
Emily Brown
Emily Burns
Emily Flicos

These people...

Emily Harris
Emily Morris
Emily Neighbour
Emily Oram-Lewis
Emily Petersen
Emily Turner
Emily Wheeler
Emma Abad
Emma Boxall
Emma Browne
Emma Clare
Emma Cooper
Emma Couch
Emma Dunn
Emma Geen
Emma Hooper
Emma Hotchkiss
Emma Matthews
Emma Rees
Emma Ritch
Emma Swann
Emmie Harrison
Erin A. Hughes
Erin Brown
Erin Sayers
Erin Slater
Esme Bailey
Esther Sparrow
Eve Livingston
Evelyn Bates
Evelyn Reinthaler
Evonne Okafor
Ewa Kulak
Fawn Colombatto
Fee Sheal

Felicity Tolley
Fenric Cayne
Fi Evans
Fi Jacobson
Finbarr Farragher
Fiona
Fiona Aleksandrowicz
Fiona Fisher
Fiona Stygall
Fiz Osborne
Flavia D'Avila
Fleur Beaupert
Floor Senda Boerwink
for Mel
Fozia Ghafoor
Fran Redmond &
Caz Vousden
Frances McAleer
Frances Sleigh
Francesca Vaney
Francesca Washtell
Francesgrace Mary-Hedwyck
Ferland
Francoise Harvey
Fraser Campbell
Fred Wilson
Freddie Harrison
Freya Barcroft
Fury Jaye
Gabrielle Brown
Gaby Calvert
Gale Wade Govro
Gary Kaill
Gary Marshall
Gem Hill

...are awesome

Gem Keyes
Gemma Elliott
Gen Shearer-McBride
Genie Ruzicka
Georgia Lennie
Georgia Murray
Georgia Odd
Georgia Smith
Georgina Rovirosa
Gerardo Alba
Gianna Dibala
Gill Hatcher
Gillian Achurch
Gillian Macrosson
Gillian Stuart
Gita Ralleigh
govy
Grace Hugueley
Graeme Macrae Burnet
Greg "schmegs" Schwartz
Hannah Bloczynski &
Alicia Jackson
Hannah Brown
Hannah Embleton-Smith
Hannah Fort-Teller
Hannah Roberts
Hannah Sheehy
Hannah Simpson
Hannah Westwater
Hara Joy
Harriet Grecian
Harry Gallon
Harry Read
Harvinder Higgens
Hayleigh Booth

Hayley Rutland-Walker
Heather Campbell
Heather Parry
Heather Turner
Heather W Britton
Hel Harding-Jones
Helen Flood
Helen Maringer
Helen McBay
Helen Murphy
Helen Sedgwick
Helen Slucher / Jane Braum
Henrica Blomqvist
Hilary Bell
Hilary Callaghan
Hilary Copeland
Hope Nicholson
Howard Kistler
Iain Mac
Iain S Ross
Ian Faddy-Widmann
Ignacio B. Peña
Ilja
Imogen McBean
Imogen Thornton-Smith
In Honour of Mary Sim
Ingrid Francis
Isabela Drabik Chaves
Isha Karki
Isobel Gillespie
Issie Tovey
J.D. Lowry
Jac Kent
Jaca Freer
Jack Semancik

These people...

Jade Esson
Jaine Heggie
Jake Dunlop
Jakki Purdon
Jalene
James Smith
James Turnbull
Jami Ann Kravec
Jamie Brown
Jamie Norman
Janahan Balasubramaniam
Jane Alexander
Jane Hanmer
Jane Lowney
Jane Simpson Anderson
Jane Smeeth
Janelle Azmy
Janet Crawford
Janina Matthewson
Janine Lawton
Jared Walther
Jarrod Phillips
Jasmine Chatfield
Jason Chen
Jason Kottler
Jen
Jen Burrows
Jen Campbell
Jen Carey
Jenna Morrison
Jenna Robertson
Jenni Hamilton
Jenni Nock
Jenni Sneddon
Jennifer Ann Corbeau

Jennifer Anne Trujillo
de Good
Jennifer Constable
Jennifer Hemphill
Jennifer Horan
Jennifer Iglesias Hernandez
Jennifer Robinson
Jennifer Vargas and Gail Vargas
Jenny Kumar
Jenny Moseley
Jenny Redhead
Jenny Scollen
Jenny Soep
Jenny Zenner
Jens Scholz
Jesay Yonan
Jeska Niemiec
Jess Anderson
Jess Glaisher
Jess Watkins
Jessica Bay
Jessica Buchanan
Jessica Rigby
Jessica Ringelstein
Jill Arthur
Jill Eshelman
Jim Knowles
Jo Bottrill
Jo Brewis
Jo Marjoribanks
Jo Pearson
Jo Reid
Joanne Bell
Jocelyn Beyer
Jodie Manning

Jodie Wilkinson
Jody Broad
Jody Eskro
Joel Boutiere
Joelle Owusu-Sekyere
John M. Osborne
John Parkes
John Pettie
Jon Raine
Jonas Oshaug Pedersen
Jonathan Schafer
Jonathan Wakeham for Gisela
Jonathan Ward
Jordan C. Roberson
Jori Bloom Naegele
Joshua Cohen
Joshua Michael Scheel
Joyce Johanna Maria Ligthart
Joyce Walker (KW)
JP
Jude Stewart
Judy Walsh
Julia Downes
Julia Geier
Julia Horvath
Julia Kate Harrison
Julie Farrell
Julie Mac
Julie Roos
Julie Vital
Julie Vuong
Juliet Robinson
Juliette Hartel
Justine Bottles
Justine Stevens

Justine Taylor
Kait Feldmann
Kala
Kara Rennie
Kari Morton
Karissa Adams
Karla J Wolff
Karyn Dougan
Kat Beadle
Kat Ford
Kat Glover
Kat Harrington
Kat Metcalf
Kate Chambers
Kate Lettin
Kate McNaughton
Kate Neilan
Kate Welshofer
Kath Butler
Katharina Vogel
Katharine
Katharine Brown
Katherine Beyer
Katherine Delzell
Katherine Hegarty
Katherine Mackinnon
Katherine Parish
Katherine Walton-Elliott
Kathleen Caskie
Kathryn Black
Kathryn van Beek
Katie Finnegan-Clarke
Katie Harrington
Katie McNicholls
Katie Rochelle-Houx

These people…

Katie West
Katy Lennon
Kay Tee
Kayla Aurora
Kayleigh Bohan
Kayleigh Pedder
Kelly Bell
Kelly Schweizer
Kelly Zimmermann
Kelsey O'Conor
Kelvin Smith
Kendra Jackson
Kendra L. Gale
Kendra Moffatt
Keri Michelle Wiley
Kerry McShane
Kev Yip
Kevin Pretterhofer
Kevin Williamson
Kiana Jane Khozein
Kiley Pole
Kim Racon
Kim Thain
Kimberly Cincilla
Kimberly M. Lowe
Kira Williams
Kirpal Bidmead
Kirsten Benecke
Kirsten Murray
Kirsten Ross
Kirsti Wishart
Kirstie Wheeler
Kirstin Lamb
Kirsty Cochrane
Kirsty Connell-Skinner

Kirsty Doole
Kirsty Fraser
Kirsty Hunter
Kirsty Logan
Kirsty McNeill
Kirsty S Hill
Kirsty Stanley
Kirsty Strickland
Kirsty W.
Kirstyn Smith
Kitty Spence
Kitty Winks
Klacie Norris
Knittingmayhem
Kris Haddow
Kristen Knight
Kristin Raphel
Kristin Rhea
Kristin Walter
Kristin, Caroline &
Meredith Reilly
Kristina Kotur
Kristina Marino
Krisztián Tóth
Kurt Boucher
Kyle Kolpek
L Doherty
Laina Tanahara
Landon Hayes Lauder
Lanie Presswood
Lara Dodds
Lassie Gaffney
Laura Anderson
Laura Autton-Wise
Laura Brevitz

...are awesome

Laura Brown
Laura Carberry
Laura Claire Elliott
Laura Clay
Laura Clements
Laura Evans
Laura Louise Smales
Laura Nessfield
Laura Stevens
Lauren & Nicola Stevenson
Lauren Ball
Lauren Howells
Lauren O'Neill
Lauren Taylor
Lawrence Ross-Bull
Layla Parchizadeh
Lee Chalmers
Lee Newell
Leigh Dunbar
Leila Essa
Leila Fouda
Leila Maria Khoshoie
Leni Rademacher
Leonie Dunlop & Amy
Todman
Lesley Barnes
Lesley Macniven
Lesley Mitchell
Liam Pritchett
Lianne Hooper
Lilith Johnstone
Lina Langlee
Linda T
Lindsay Millar
Lindis Kipp

Lindsey Arneson–Moody
Lindsey Millen
Linnea Jones
Lis "Last Year's Girl" Ferla
Lisa Jenkins
Lisa Marie Shepherd
Lisa McCurrach
Livvy J Hooper
Liz Fox
Lizzie Kaye
Lizzy Maries
Logan Marlowe
Lois Wilson-McFarland
Loraine Williams
Loren
Lori England
Lorna Mackinnon
Lorraine Hamilton
Louie Stowell
Louise Corcoran
Louise Hare
Louise Kavanagh
Louise Marie
Louise O'Neill
Louise Weinzweig
Love Sex, Hate Sexism
Collective
LSindt
Luci Wallace
Lucy Goodwill
Lucy Kelsall
Lucy Kenny
Lucy Llewellyn
Lucy McGhee
Lucy R. Hinnie

These people...

Lux
Lydia Crow
Lydia Gittins
Lyla Serenity Rose Hansford
Lyndsay Coleman
Lyndsey Seaborn
Lynn Charles
Lynsey Robbie
Lynsey Smith
M. E. Mitchell
MA Creative Writing @
Edinburgh Napier
Maddy Howell
Madelaine Moore
Madeleine van Adrighem
Madeline Francis
Madison Atkins
Maegan Garland
Maegan Springman and
Carly Nicholson
Magda Pieta
Mahan Harirsaz
Mairead Loftus
Mairi Claire Hubbard
Mairi McKay
Mairi Skinner
Maize Wallin
Maja Baek
Majda Gama
Majo Espinosa
Malarie Burgess
Malcolm Chisholm
Malik Ahmad
Malin Christina Wikström
Manuela Cerri Goren

Margaux Vialleron
Margot McCuaig
Maria Moore
Mariah Busher
Marian Pérez-Santiago
Marianne MacRae
Marie Barnett
Marilyn Kyle
Marina
Marine Furet
Marissa D
Marie Leadbetter
Marjorie Lotfi Gill
Mark Beechill
Mark Bolsover
Mark Chandler
Mark Leggatt
Mark Nixon
Mark Wightman
Marta Bausells
Martin Baxter
Martin Sellner IBÖ
Mary Hanora O'Sullivan
Mary Ormerod
Mary Paulson-Ellis
Mary Young
Maureen Murray
Maxine Blane
Maxine Davies
Meadhbh Ryan
Meagan Tanti
Mediah Ahmed
Megan Bethke
Megan Bull
Megan Duffy Cassella

Megan Reid
Melanie McAinsh
Melanie Lisa Smith
Melinda Salisbury
Melissa Brydon
Melissa Hugel
Melissa Jackowski
Michaela Zikmundová
Michael Höhne
Michael Stec
Michael Swift
Michali Dawn Hyams
Michelle Labbé
Michelle Martir
Mika Cook
Mike Inglis
Mike Murphy
Milena Iciek
Miles
Miranda Hlady
Miranda Murphy
Mo & Sepp
Moira Findlay
Molly Ann Monahan
Molly Gibb
Monica Burns
Monika Kanokova
Morven Dooner
Morven Gow
Muireann Crowley
Mullissa Willette
Murray Robertson
Nadia Phipps
Nadia Suchdev
Nadim Mamoojee

Nancy B Rugen
Naomi Carson
Naomi Frisby
Naomi Jane Peel
Natalie Fergie
Natalie Novick
Natalie Ohlson
Natalie Poernig
Natasha R. Chisdes
Nathalie Pham
Neil Hargreaves
Nermeen Zia
Nia Jackson-Owens
Nic Kipar
Nick Mellish
Nicola Balkind
Nicola Day
Nicolai Schwarz
Nicolas Longtin-Martel
Nicole Brandon
Nicole Colton
Nicole Sweeney
Nicole True
Nikesh Shukla
Nikki Bi
Nikki Jewell
Nikki Murphy
Nivea
Noel Johnson
Noura Alzuabi
Nyla Ahmad
Olga Wojtas
Olivia McCarthy
Olivia Rose French
Olivia Sime

These people...

Olusola
Orlaith Bermingham
Pablo P.
Paige Bromley
Paige Kimble
Pamela Berry
Pat Wilken
Patric Geissbuehler
Patricia G Sparks
Patricia Lomax
Patricia S.
Patrick Nickell
Paul Benton
Paul Decker
Paul Loveland
Paul Michaels
Paul Philbin
Pauline Reinhardt
Peggy Hughes
Penny Haddrill
Pete Taylor
Petra Pavlikova
Petya Yakimova
Polly Brownlee
Poppy Peacock
Poppy Starkie
Preeti Desai
Priscilla Looi
Priya Shah
QR
R Laurenson
R. Moore
Rachael Laburn
Rachael North
Rachael Powers

Rachel A.N. Brewer
Rachel Attewell
Rachel F Smith
Rachel Kelsey
Rachel McCann
Rachel McCrum
Rachel Nye
Rachel Patrick
Rachel Samuel
Rachel Shapira
Rae Kershaw
Rafael Pacheco
Raúl
Ray
Rebecca Bonallie
Rebecca Eira Ferguson
Rebecca Faith Carroll
Rebecca Grieser
Rebecca Hunter
Rebecca Junell
Rebecca Preib
Rebecca Smith
Renee K Y Chin
Rhiannon Howe
Rhiannon Lock
Rhona Togher
Ria Cagampang
Ricky Monahan Brown
RikRak & SunBun
Rishaad Moudden
Rishi Dastidar
Riyaz Talkhani
Rob Crowther
Rob Giddings
Rob Williams

Robbie Guillory
Robinina and the ladies
of the BE Hive
Robyn Donoghue
Rochelle Domingo
Róisín O'Brien
Ros O'Sullivan
Rose O'Keefe
Roseanne Watt
Rosie Earl
Rosie Howie
rosiecanning1@gmail.com
Rosita Pederzolli
Ross Dixon
Ross McCleary
Ross Sayers
Ross Williams
Rotem Raviv
Rowan Hisayo Buchanan
Rowena Knight
Ruth and Maria
Ruth Bennett
Ruth Boreham
Ruth Lillian Foulis
Ruthie Morgan
Ryan De Freitas
S L Puma
Sabrina Maguire
Sabrina-Delphine S.
Saima Mir
Saisree Cherukuri
Salim Mamoojee
Sally E. Foster
Sally Huband
Sally R. Baxter

Sam Bradley
Sam Clark
Sam Gimbel
Samantha Missingham
Samantha Shannon
Samya Kelly
Sapphire Bleach
Sara Co
Sara Harrington
Sara Hunt
Sara Zo
Sarah Agterhuis
Sarah Anne Medearis
Sarah Barnard
Sarah Creed
Sarah E M Mason
Sarah Emery
Sarah Garnham
Sarah Helena Burgess
Sarah Leviseur
Sarah Losofsky-Barron
Sarah Lough
SarahLouise McDonald
Sarah Morrison
Sarah Pybus
Sarah Robinson
Sarah Rouse
Sarah Sandow
Sarah Shields
Sarah Wilford
Sarah-Anne Forteith
Savannah Lang
Saz
Sean Cleaver
Sean Curran

These people…

Seangelina of AK
Sebastian Gilits
Sebastian Ossowski
Seonaid MacLeod
Seonaid Rogers
Sevrina Flores
Shane Strachan
Shannon Dooley
Shannon J
Sharon Bussey-Reschka
Shawn Ta
Shehzar DojaHanna
Shelby Voeltz
Shiona
Shireen Taylor
Shiva Kumar
Shohini Shome
Si Paton
Sian Cain
Sian Peters
Sibyl Adam
Sid Orlando
Simay Bayatli
Sileas Wood
Simon
Simon Savidge
Simon William Cree
Sinéad Grainger
Sinéad Scully
Siobhan Shields
Sonia Sandhu
Sonya Adams
Sonya Lalli
Sophie Cameron
Sophie FT

Sophie Hiscox Paterson
Sophie Mayer
Sophie Reid
Spencer Chou
Stacey Walton
Stacy M Nelson
Stefani Sloma
Stefania Lamprinidi
Stefanie McCartney
Stella and Derek Birrel
Steph Pomfrett
Stephanie Griffin
Stephanie J Mitchell
Stephanie Osorio
Stephanie Trier
Stephen C. Ward
Stephen Keyes
Stephen Wills
Steve Heller-Murphy
Steve Nicoll
Stevie Louise Marsden
Stew Dobbs
Storm Patterson
Stuart Chaplin
Stuart Pyper
Stuart Sim
Suki Chall
Susan Berridge
Susan Feiner
Susan Tardif
Susannah Cooke
Susie McIvor
Susie Murray
Susmita Bhattacharya
Suvi Heusala

Suzanne Connor
Suzey Ingold
Suzie Brady
Suzy Mosedale
Swedian Lie
Tabassum Mamoojee
Tabi Joy
Tammy S
Tanner Blackwell
Tanya Byrne
Tara Birch
Tara Quinn
Tatiana
Tatjana Herold
Teddy Graham
Teri Powell
Terra Byrne
Terri-Jane Dow
Tess & Kate Hutchison
Thane Bevan Elders
The people of 7 Foden Street
The Screever Lee
Theresa Blakesley
Thom Cuell
Thomas Closs
Thomas Liljeruhm
Thomas Pickles
Tian Zheng
Tiffany Grimston
Tiffany Jang Lydia Sochurek
Timothy C. Baker
Tiril Pollard
TJ Matthews
Tom Delfino
Tom Ryan

Tonje Hefte
Tori Hansen
Tracy Pehar
Tricia Copeland
Tristan Beer
Trystan Vel
Tutku TUTS Barbaros
Tyler Corsair
Tyler Robertson
Valeria Villegas Lindvall
Vanessa Murphy
Veronique Kootstra
Viccy Adams
Vicki Jarrett
Vicky Hobbs
Vicky Ingram
Victoria Culbertson
Victoria Halsam
Victoria McFadyen
Victoria Sinden
Vikki Reilly
Virginia Bemis
Vonny Moyes
Wendy Kelleher
Wendy Tuxworth
Will McInnes
Willa Köerner
William Bruce
William Trimby
Z Hay
Zainab Juma
Zoe Flatman
Zoe Ford
Zoe MacLeod
Zoe Mitchell

ABOUT 404 INK

404 Ink is a new, alternative and independent book and literary magazine publisher based in the UK. We look to publish the weirder and wilder fiction, non-fiction, poetry and comics out there in our magazine, in English, Scots and Scottish Gaelic. New issues are released in November and May every year. You can subscribe to the magazine through Patreon (find us at www.patreon.com/404ink) or buy single issues from our website (below).

We're always on the lookout for novels, short story collections, narrative non-fiction, and graphic novels and we accept unsolicited submissions. Drop by our website for full information on submissions and more: www.404ink.com

Find/follow/like us at all the usual places:

Facebook: /404ink
Twitter: @404ink
Instagram: 404ink

hello@404ink.com